DOCTOR IN MIND

A Guide to understanding how your Doctor thinks

CONTENTS

PREFACE

Doctors are always talking about being "patient-centred". There are even tools to tell us how patient-centred we are. It has a simple meaning at heart – how much time and effort do we invest in each consultation to try and meet the patient on their own terms? We spend hours learning how to communicate with patients. We take examinations designed to test this.

It all seems so unfair –isn't about time patients learnt how to communicate with doctors? Medical Schools teach students to speak "medical" – it's almost a new language. It's only recently that it has been openly recognised that patients generally don't speak "Medical". Typically, the profession has described this in a "Medical" term calling it Health Literacy. This is a wide concept but essentially it is about levelling the playing field so both doctor and patient are speaking the same language.

When I have discussed with colleagues that it was about time we told patients what and how we're thinking with how and why we're behaving they have reacted with horror – "you can't tell them that!"

So – with apologies to those colleagues – this book aims to do just that. I want to explore why doctors consult patients the way they do and how patients can make a consultation more effective by understanding us better. The academics might say your Health Literacy will increase. I hope the result will be better care, and perhaps a few laughs on the way

I had planned to stop writing after the first section but, as I wrote, I realised some budding Doctors might read this book. I'd be delighted if they did, particularly if they became GPs! So, I've added a final section which describes what sort of career a GP can have. It does not begin to convey the breadth of interests many of my fellow GPs have and General Practice remains the medical career option that best allows Doctors to express their individuality. I have thoroughly enjoyed my career and if 1 young person reads this and gives it a go I will be cock-a-hoop!

INTRODUCTION

J im had a pain in his ear – not really "in" but more "on" his ear. It started a few months ago and was really painful. It seemed ridiculous that all he had to show for all this pain was a small swelling that was barely even red. It was now waking him up every time he turned over in bed and Judith, his wife, was not having that. She'd made him an appointment to see Dr Roberts. She said his snoring was bad enough without this.

"You've got Chondrodermatitis Nodularis Chronicis Helicis" said Dr Roberts. "Wow" thought Jim "these doctors really know their stuff". He was reassured by the authoritative way this diagnosis was delivered to him – 4, or was it 5, unpronounceable, seriously impressive words. Sally would be staggered when he told her - if he could remember any of the words!

Dr Roberts smiled to himself - in his medical student days the skin specialist had added another word - Chondrodermatitis Nodularis Chronicis Helicis Dolores. He was then a 20 years old medical student and was just as impressed as Jim was now. Since then he had learnt that this was 1 of the many tricks doctors had got up to for centuries. He usually waited for the looks of surprise, wonder, awe and confusion to settle and then explained. "*Chondro* is just the prefix for cartilage (perhaps we should call it gristle –the rubbery stuff your ear is made of). *Derm* is the same for skin and *itis* just means inflamed ie arthritis means inflamed joints, tonsillitis means inflamed tonsils, balanitis means…well perhaps we'll stop there.

Nodularis means like a nodule, chronica means it's been there awhile and helicis means of the ear.

So you told me you had a swelling on your ear that's a bit red and has been there a few months and hurts. I called it Chondrodermatitis Nodularis Chronicis Helicis Dolores. Exactly the same thing but in Latin! It doesn't mean I understand what it is or why you have it. I don't: no-one does. But boy does it sound clever!

That same skin specialist (dermatologist if we are into making impressions with words) was a bit of a stickler for being precise – she called it Chondrodermatitis Nodularis Chronicis *Anti-*Helicis Dolores – anatomically correct but a step too far for Dr Roberts' Latin.

I have spent hours in my career teaching consultation skills to doctors and students and have only recently realised that I've been missing a crucial point. Isn't it about time patients learnt how to communicate with doctors? I have met quite a few doctors in my career where this is a real challenge.

So here we are – this book aims to tell you, the patient, what your doctor is thinking, what techniques (or tricks?) he or she is using to get you to spill the beans as quickly as possible so they can see the next patient before the 10 minutes is over. All this whilst making you feel listened to, taken seriously and dealt with appropriately. That is what makes the role of a GP such a challenge and even a joy!

We are going to follow Jim, his family and some of his friends through the medical minefields of life as they see Dr Roberts and some of his colleagues at the Piper St Surgery.

This book carries a medical warning - if you read it you might never quite see your doctor in the same light again!

PART 1

Family Medicine

THE PEOPLE WE'LL MEET

Robert..............the GP

Moses...............the GP Registrar

Brian................the Great Grandad

Jim....................Grandad, Brian's son

Judith...............Grandma, Jim's wife

Sally...................Jim and Judith's daughter

Molly.................Sally's partner

Tara...................the baby

Lora...................the Bulgarian

SALLY

D octor Roberts was getting ready for his next patient. He was actually christened Robert Roberts: parents often seem to have strange ideas when deciding on names, he felt. Patients generally called him Dr Roberts and he preferred it this way. Friends know him as Robert. Some patients called him Bob. Most did this in a sort of friendly intimacy and he let it pass. Some were frankly trying to manipulate him but both were wrong. He was not and had never been called Bob – his mother would turn in her grave, if she hadn't been cremated that was.

He had noticed how Medical Students were now being trained to introduce themselves and often said "My name is Angela, how would you like me to address you?" Interesting that they almost always used their first name not realising that this pressured the patient into doing the same. Not many of his patients, mainly the older ones, wanted their doctor on first names terms he felt but perhaps he was becoming old-fashioned along with them. Like most doctors he had pondered about this on many occasions and a degree of formality seemed to suit him. He was very fond of most of his patients but they were not really friends. How many friends would he like to see through the trauma of miscarriage, tell them they had advanced cancer, watch them die? Some distance here seemed wise to him. But horses for courses he thought, not all doctors are the same.

The next patient was Sally Martin. He looked at his ever-present companion these days. The computer. She was 26 years old, the computer reminded him he had met her before but only for minor illness and contraception. One of the joys of General Practice was that a patient could come through the door and surprise you. There were almost limitless possibilities from top to toe. Their symptoms might mean very little, or very much. He sometimes, rather melodramatically perhaps, felt like a medical Sherlock Holmes.

"All fertile women are pregnant until proved otherwise". One of the myriad pearls of wisdom his Professors at Medical School had given him. He called Sally in on the tannoy. It took her about 30 seconds to reach his door, about average. Too quick might suggest anxiety, too slow perhaps poor mobility or serious illness. No response usually meant they were in the toilet, or deaf! In that 30 seconds he noticed she was due a cervical cancer smear (her first) and no-one had recorded whether she smoked or her Body mass index. In the bottom right of his computer screen he had what he called his "nagging box". In 2004 the NHS introduced a performance related pay system. GPs had to collect points which were awarded for a record of illness and levels of care. Recording things like smoking status, height and weight were included. If you reached a critical percentage of points (perhaps 70%) then Bingo – you were paid more. There were more than 1000 points. Most GPs had very mixed feelings about this system. It seemed to encourage computer-watching and distracted doctors from the issues the patient wanted to discuss, particularly when there are only 10 minutes to work with. Personally, Dr Roberts had a deep antipathy for his computer, it was an almost personal hatred. He remembered life "BC". Before Computers. His computer often misbehaved and his staff, affectionately he hoped, called these PICNIC problems. Problem-In-Chair-Not-In-Computer was sadly often right! He realised, with a little petulance, that he was not Canute and that there were *some* benefits. He had moved the computer out of his eye-line, positioned the patient's chair away from the computer and he tried to turn away from the beckoning screen at least for the first few minutes.

Sally knocked, as most patients still do, and came in. "Hello Mrs Martin, come in and sit down, how can I help?" Robert could never forget a colleague he knew whilst he was training. He was young, enthusiastic and popular. He had decided to experiment with the seating arrangements in his room to see where the patient might like to sit particularly in relation to his own chair. Doctors in the past often sat across a big imposing status-symbol desk in a large chair with the patient opposite, often on a smaller chair. The doctor was asserting their power. The patient knew where they stood, or should sit at least. That was a rare arrangement these days, but Kieran (the colleague in mind) was keen to see what his patients might like. He would stand at reception and direct the patients to his room asking them to take a seat and he'd be down in a minute. He had placed about 4 chairs in the room in various orientations to his own- alongside, opposite, closer, further away etc. After a week Robert asked him how it was going. "I've given up" he said, "When I go to the room most of the patients are standing there scratching their heads and wondering where to sit". Robert went with the slightly alongside, across the corner of the desk approach.

Robert had opted for a simple opening. He wondered whether patients realised how much time GPs spent thinking about this opener. Should I use a different phrase for different patients? What about introducing myself, almost all patients now know me well so it seems silly? What do I say to encourage the patient? "How are you?" (over-used as a social greeting perhaps) "What's the problem?" (somehow a bit too direct and limiting) "What are we doing today" (bit vague?) "How can I help?" seemed OK this time. He had been known to use "What are you doing here?" and even "Oh no not you again". They were for particular patients where he knew he'd get away with it!

Sally sat down. She had been rehearsing what to say in the waiting room. Robert knew research confirmed this. GPs called this first phrase the Curtain Raiser. It was often a bland statement that served to get the conversation going. "what a nice/ wet/ frosty/snowy/sunny/horrible day it is" was common. So was "Your tannoy is awful" (it was) "the waiting room is very full" occasionally and, when he had a room at the end of the building, it was almost always "that's a long corridor". The next phrase is often still short but is usually laden with meaning. It contains either direct or sometimes indirect clues to what the whole consultation will be about. He thought of a recent patient he'd seen whose second statement, his Opening Gambit as it had become known as, was "My wife thinks you should take a look at a spot I've got, her uncle had a serious one removed recently". It was a patient he did not know but these 20 words told him so much. The obvious stuff – he was married, he had a "spot" causing concern and a relative with a "spot" too. He felt awkward coming in case it was seen as a trivial problem so was using his wife to explain why he was there. He either did not know (unlikely) that the Uncle's spot was cancer or was reluctant to use the word. Having a relative with a probable cancer heightens bodily awareness so this might just be an anxiety issue. Why is his wife concerned? Has she some knowledge? Has she been googling?

"I've missed a period" Sally said. She was looking directly at Robert, no trace of anxiety, the tone of the phrase was neutral and she stopped at this point. Robert was thinking: She hadn't suggested she was pregnant, perhaps she thought that was his job. Perhaps she had done a pregnancy test already but felt a bit embarrassed to say this (her notes suggested she was on the contraceptive pill). He couldn't even assume she would be pleased with a pregnancy - she might be about to request a termination. He needed to find a similarly neutral phrase to encourage her to continue. He knew that research suggested patients need only 1-2 minutes usually to "spill the beans" and that GPs had a bit of a tendency to leap in and take control of the conversation after only 20 or 30 seconds. He had been taught about Open and Closed questions. Open questions "Can you tell me a bit more about that" encourage the patient to talk. Closed questions "How long has that been going on for?" often produce short staccato conversations and inhibit a more free-flowing interaction.

"Do you think you might be pregnant?" Robert asked, laughing inwardly that his old professor's maxim might be spot on this time. "Well we have been trying for the last month or 2 but I felt it took longer usually" Sally said smilingly. Robert smiled back but said nothing. Sally seemed to be a bit of a short-sentence patient and he thought silence might encourage her to say more. "Nature abhors a vacuum" sprang to mind - generally humans abhor silence and simply keeping shtum encouraged them. That was as long as they weren't better than he was at tolerating the quiet! Sally had smiled, revealed she suspected she was pregnant and had expressed a Health Belief. This was doctor jargon: health beliefs are essentially indications of how the patient thinks health and disease work. They are an endless source of amusement for doctors. You can't get pregnant after sex standing up, apple seeds are bad for you: they wrap around your heart, if a shingles rash reaches your middle you'll die. The list is endless, and potentially endlessly amusing. Some are based on ancient old wives' tales. Robert often thought these probably had some validity - Phlegm is "better out than in" might not be evidence-based medicine but it was probably sound advice. Sally's health belief was more straightforward. She thought conception took a while and generally she was right. Robert told her it often took up to a year (after all even that is only 12 tries) and the average was about 6-9 months but she must be good at it! That made Sally smile in a slightly anxious manner.

"How are you feeling?" asked Robert with another open question opening his body posture to encourage Sally more. He had spent many hours learning and teaching Non-verbal communication skills. Most people are surprised to hear that most of the meaning of any interaction is conveyed in this way. Very little comes from the actual words used. Body position, eye contact, mirroring mannerisms, facial expressions were all tools of the trade. Then there were the paralinguistic elements; The tone, delivery, phraseology and paraphraseology. Robert regularly used his body posture to help patients relax, some might say to even coerce them into relaxation. By using a gentle tone of voice, pacing the delivery of his inquiries and deliberately re-using aspects of the patient's vocabulary he was creating an atmosphere where patients could drop their normal social guard. If a patient had a "prickly oozing pain" then asking them about this later and using the same words created a feeling of understanding and empathy. Robert had read 1 or 2 books on Neurolinguistic Programming or NLP for short. This was a system of communication initially developed in the world of marketing to allow American retailers to get customers to buy their product. It had evolved into a widely used, and marketed, set of communication tools. He found the VAK aspects of it useful. Patients (and doctors) have a range of Visual, Auditory or Kinaesthetic approaches to thinking that are expressed in their behaviour and communication. Most patients have a preference for V or A or K and by getting to know them and listening carefully Robert could assess this preference. He had done courses where you could actually complete assessments that told you your VAK preferences. Once you had the idea then you could use an approach that matched the patient's preference and this was a powerful tool for creating a sense of empathy in the patient. Patients often had visual preferences so he could "see what they meant". Sally had shaken his hand as she entered (a bit unusual in this age group) and had used a few *feeling* words. She had responded well to his re-use of the word feeling and he thought probably had a significant kinaesthetic preference. He remembered reading about eye movements and how they could also indicate mind states. He had even tried to use these for a while putting a covert sheet of which movements meant what on the strut of a shelf but it hadn't stuck. Either on the shelf or in his mind! The only ones he remembered were the large movements that indicated visual, auditory or kinaesthetic memories that could sometimes prompt him to ask a matched question like "How does that make you feel?" or "I can't quite see what you mean?" Some doctors became Masters of NLP, Robert felt he dabbled. In his more philosophical moments he wondered where good communication stopped and manipulation began. Sometimes these techniques tripped patients' defences: was this ethical? He reassured himself that positive intent and the old Hippocratic "Primum non Nocere" (First do no harm) were appropriate defences.

Sally revealed she had done 2 positive pregnancy tests. Robert had known women do 3,4,5 or 6 (his record was 10) tests – all positive! Some felt the "cheap" ones might not be reliable but he thought generally it was the need to be sure particularly as most women seemed to expect to *feel* pregnant in some way when they didn't feel different at all. "Congratulations" Robert said "When was the first day of your last period?" Time for the closed questions to gather the information he needed. This was an essential piece of information. Antenatal care is based around this date and Robert always asked with a slight air of trepidation. It could provoke frantic diary searching or prolonged debate over his own calendar - "well it was after the dog had puppies and before my Hen Night". Sometimes it drew a complete blank and somehow was impossible to define. Sally was more organised "the 5th April" she said. "So, you're due on the 12th Jan" said Robert immediately. He couldn't remember who taught him the quick calculation trick and it did depend on a 28-day cycle. He always expected patients to be impressed by his speed of thought (actually you just add 7 days and take off 3 months) but they rarely were! "That's what I thought" said Sally. In the youth of his career he had dallied with predicting sex. With a 1 in 2 chance he was right 50% of the time and it seemed if he was right patients remembered and if he was wrong they forgot. He had quite a reputation as a sex predicting oracle but had grown a few grey hairs since and now saw this as a youthful aberration.

Communication Courses over many years had introduced Robert to Connecting skills, Establishing rapport, the verbal handshake and many more concepts. The techniques behind these phrases had become part of Robert's consultation style and allowed him to create the relationships that were at the core of his Practice. If he could not make that particular patient feel his interest, concern, competence and care then things would probably not go well for either of them. Sally had come with a "nice" problem with no diagnostic uncertainty, no complex issues, a positive outcome in a well and happy patient. This was an "easy" consultation. It still took at least 10 minutes to cover all the areas for a mother to be. All the do's and don'ts of early pregnancy, discussing delivery preferences, arranging antenatal care, a quick examination and then the notes and letters. Sally actually left after 9 minutes, clutching a booklet on pregnancy, a website address, a prescription for folic acid and a midwife referral. And a little smile.

As she left Robert reflected on a dimension he felt his old tutors, good as they had been, had missed. He felt that GPs needed to be interested, motivated and knowledgeable but they also, quaint as it may seem, needed to find something they liked in every patient. Usually this was easy but on rare occasions it was a real challenge. "Everyone loves their mother" was his own bottom line and reminded him to look for the likeable that was present in everyone. So far life had not let him down.

In his own experience patients were keenly sensitive to this aspect of their relationship with doctors. It seemed more important than clinical acumen, good prescribing or even good communication skills. Sadly, he heard patients say "they just didn't seem to care" which was surely the worst condemnation for any doctor.

JUDITH

J udith was having pain. She was 52 now and felt she'd probably has these pains off and on for a few years. But this was different. After the curry she'd had last week she'd been up all night in agony. Time to see a doctor.

Robert was having a nice morning. It was a nice sunny day and nothing too taxing as yet. A number of his regulars for review of their high blood pressure, diabetes or depression and most seemed as sunny as the weather. He remembered a Chinese study years ago saying the phases of the moon affected health. It was a full moon last night: perhaps they were right! If the moon can move the oceans perhaps it can move people too, he mused. Judith was his first "urgent" appointment today. Like many Practices some slots were kept for the day to try and meet the need for more acute illness. Unfortunately, no-one seemed to have ever really defined what Urgent meant. Patients were confused - often when they made the decision to see a doctor it was urgent in their own mind. Even if the symptoms had been going on weeks, months or even sometimes years! Some of the "regular" patients got to understand the system and would always say it was urgent. This could make it difficult for acutely ill patients to see a doctor. Robert had seen all sorts of appointment systems over the years, even some practices with no apparent system at all! There was no perfect solution here and he had learned not to get too worked up by it all.

Robert greeted Judith with a smile and a direct look. Judith had prepared herself. Robert listened to the "History of the presenting complaint" as it had been first described to him many years ago. As Judith told her story he was reminded of the mnemonics he first heard as a student. Sally had blonde hair, was 46, had 3 children and was a bit plump. Fair, fat, fertile, female and forty to fifty. Judith had a right sided severe, colicky pain in her abdomen that lasted hours and was worse after a fatty meal. She couldn't understand why her shoulder seemed to ache with it too. All this was adding up to typical gall bladder pain and likely gall stones Robert thought. Patients were often confused by "referred" pain. Robert explained: "Generally humans get pain in the area that has the problem – but not always. As a result of how we evolved and are formed in the womb certain areas of the body seem to have illogical connections. A pain in your toes can be because a nerve is irritated in your back. The gallbladder can irritate your diaphragm and the nerve to this area shares connections to your shoulder - so you feel the pain there". Robert still re-membered many of the mnemonics from his Medical School days – some he wished he didn't recall! Medical students were not always "PC" and certainly not in the 1970's. He was taught about the 12 cranial nerves: Olfactory, Optic, Oculomotor, Trochlea, Trigeminal, Abducent, Facial, Auditory, Glossopharyngeal, Vagus, Accessory, Hypoglossal. Almost all students (male and female) used a pneumonic he would now hesitate to repeat: Oh, Oh, Oh To Touch And Feel A ... perhaps best to stop there he considered. Recently he heard students are only taught about 5 or 6 of the nerves. Perhaps that was better! There are 8 bones in the wrist – but that mnemonic was even worse and had to be forgotten quickly he thought! Students still use mnemonics – even officially. SOCRATES is used to ask patients about pain: Site, Onset, Character, Radiation, Asso-ciation, Timing, Exacerbating/relieving factors and Severity. Much more modern he felt.

Robert rapidly decided gallstones were highly likely here and started to discuss this with Judith. He had never been taught about how doctors make diagnostic decisions as a student but this was now part of most Medical School courses. Robert had read about techniques that he now recognised in his own practice. Sometimes a patient will describe a distinctly recognisable pattern of symptoms. Judith had done just that. Throughout training and through experience Robert's brain had coded these patterns allowing him to match them to her symptoms and make a diagnosis. Robert recalled that the word diagnosis means to "tell apart". If he made his mind up quickly without considering alternatives this was not "diagnosis". Most patients required the "hypothetical-deductive" approach. Research revealed that a doctor is generating a list of possible diagnoses within a few minutes of the consultation. He knew that this list is usually limited by the capacity of the human brain and is rarely more than 5 to 7 possibilities. The doctor refines this list by collecting information that makes each possibility more or less likely. When he went to Medical School Robert had naively expected to be taught exactly how likely each symptom would predict disease ie coughing up blood would indicate a 10% chance of lung cancer. He had been disappointed to find out that these sorts of precise figures were not available and that the real world was much more complicated. As time passed, and some of these predictive figures began to appear in the literature, he realised this might make his diagnostic skills redundant. However, he remained reassured by research that doctors still seemed to be better at diagnosis than computers – most of the time anyway. In some cases, Robert was at a loss for any diagnosis. This might be for a whole host of reasons. He might not have enough knowledge or experience. Maybe this was a rare diagnosis and he'd never seen it before. Maybe he was having an off-day today. Maybe the patient was a "poor historian" and was not able to give him a coherent or complete history despite his efforts. Robert had always seen diagnosis like a jigsaw. He collected the pieces, put them together carefully, and the picture emerged. He might not need all the pieces to see the picture. Sometimes the picture was a jumble and then he needed to keep collecting more pieces. This involved a more systematic approach to taking the patient's history, perhaps investigations, perhaps asking a colleague or even referring the patient.

Robert remembered his first science teacher telling him about OPHET. This had stuck in his 12-year old mind as a good approach to problem solving. What are we Observing? (the patient's story here) What is the

Problem? (the list of diagnoses and treatments), What is the Hypothesis? (the diagnosis you are going to go with), How can you test (Experiment) this to develop your Theory? (the probable best way forward). It reminded Robert of a phrase he had heard although he did not remember its origin – Good doctors try to destroy their diagnoses. It was the medical version of the scientific principle that any theory should be tested to destruction. If it survived it was probably right.

Robert had recently come across a description of what were termed "Thought Traps". He recognised these in his own experience. They were the pitfalls of the human brain and he felt awareness of them helped him make fewer mistakes. Sometimes the diagnosis was made too quickly – perhaps because of time pressures that were a daily feature of NHS practice. "The Premature Closure" trap was one you could fall into easily. It looks like A so it must be A (even if B is actually more likely if you just listened a bit longer). Sometimes the symptoms seem to be pointing in a particular direction and the doctor enthusiastically heads off that way. Unfortunately, the patient quietly mentions something that changes that direction in an instant, or should have done. The doctor is in the "Investment Trap" and is so determined they must be right they ignore this critical piece of information. Robert particularly liked the "Superiority Trap". I'm the doctor so I must be right! He remembered a survey of anaesthetists where 92% thought they were above average performers! When faced with uncertainty it could be easy to fall into this trap as a defence mechanism. Robert also liked the word assume. He had seen all sorts of problems arise out of assumptions. They generally made an ASS out of U and ME. He tried to be surer of his own assumptions.

Making a secure diagnosis and planning a way forward with the patient, usually without a battery of tests and a team of other people seeing the patient, is a real challenge for the GP. Most patients do not appreciate that medicine varies considerably in relation to its context. Robert thought this was best summarised by the renowned GP Marshall- Marinker:

Consultants   Reduce uncertainty

Explore possibility

Marginalise risk

GPs   Tolerate uncertainty

Explore probability

Marginalise danger

He wondered how the health service would develop if GPs adopted the consultant approach where the numbers of investigations and referrals would spiral as more and more cases were explored to exclude unlikely disease, with all the added costs, anxiety, resources and even pain that this would entail.

Robert asked Judith to lie on the couch. He thought patients expected him to examine them but remembered a quotation, (He thought it was from Sir William Osler who seemed to have made a myriad of them) going something like "if a physician has not made a diagnosis after talking to the patient, he is unlikely to make one after examining them". He had struggled with examination techniques as a student. Some people could hear murmurs he couldn't, some could feel a spleen he couldn't, some even see rashes that didn't seem to be there! It took several years for him to realise the subjective nature of most examination findings. He remembered a Professor asking him to examine a hernia in his final examination. The Professor asked whether it was a direct or indirect hernia. Now there was a textbook answer for this and Robert knew it. He also knew a study published that week had shown that Consultants could not tell the difference! He took the easy way out and gave the book answer. The Professor was not one to disagree with and this seemed the safest approach. He passed the exam! Examination felt like a bit of a dark art - something of the laying on of hands or the healing touch about it and not strictly an objective clinical process. Sometimes patients seemed to think he had "x ray" hands (perhaps MRI hands these days), more Paul Daniels or Dynamo than physician. Clinical signs (as doctors call examination findings) could sometimes be crucial but were often technically unnecessary to make a secure diagnosis. He remembered a doctor who had forgotten his stethoscope and, realising the patient was expecting a chest examination, took out a coin from his pocket and placed it on the back of the patient's chest. "Breathe in, breathe out" he then said. Probably an apocryphal story he thought. He also recalled a patient who denied he had examined their chest even in the face of his findings being recorded in the notes. It transpired that he had examined the back of the chest (with his stethoscope, not a coin!), findings being much more likely here, and the patient did not see this as her chest. In the days when Robert had given first aid lessons to good old British Rail staff, he taught basic anatomy by having a large chalk image of a body on the blackboard. He invited people to draw organs in and it was amazing what people would draw. Usually the lungs would start as 2 tennis ball sized organs in the chest enlarged a little with some prompting – perhaps to large orange size. Robert would then ask what else was in the chest and finally have them enlarged to all but fill the chest cavity. He remembered one smart Alec who had been there the year before at the same session. He rather smugly stepped forward to volunteer expecting perhaps the bladder, heart or even liver as his task. Robert couldn't resist: "The pineal gland please" he said handing him the chalk. Not so smug after that and a bit cruel perhaps.

He found no signs in Judith's abdomen. He didn't really expect to. An ultrasound scan confirmed gallstones and 3 months later they were removed. Judith had a curry to celebrate.

JUDITH

This wasn't fair. Judith had only just had her gallbladder removed and hadn't bargained on seeing another doctor for at least a year. But twice in a week now and she was worried. The first time was just a streak of blood and she tried to ignore that. She didn't even mention it to Jim. Talking about your bowels wasn't the most romantic of subjects after all. But today there had been a real gush and she felt it needed checking.

Robert saw Judith in one of his urgent slots. Some of his colleagues got very upset when receptionists gave patients these appointments for what seemed like non-urgent issues. Robert had seen nappy rashes, symptoms that had been present for months and even a request for a "golf buggy note" (to allow him to use the buggy on the course for medical reasons) in "urgent" slots. He remembered his barber (actually their all hairdressers now he noted), who was very good at talking (aren't they all he also noted), saying how, as far as he was concerned if he needed to see a doctor it was always urgent! He remembered being taught that patients only really came for 1 of 2 reasons: they had either reached the limit of their anxiety about a symptom or the problem they had was starting to limit their lifestyle. Perhaps it wasn't too surprising if patients see both of those as urgent. He mused that few patients really understood the difference between urgent and important.

"Hello Judith. How are the curries these days?" Robert started. Judith and Robert shared a smile. He often used this technique as his own curtain raiser. He was sure it made patients feel he remembered them in particular. One had actually answered "Wow you've got a good memory" and he had smiled at that too. Patients might be surprised at what is written in their notes. Robert often recorded where they were going on holiday, what book they were reading, details of their interests or hobbies as well as the usual stuff on what job they did, the kids names etc. Simply by having a quick look at the notes he could prime himself. Was this disingenuous? He felt it helped place him back in the patient's life and they were useful aides-memoires to make this possible.

"Oh, that's fine now" replied Judith "But I have another problem now – I've been bleeding from down below". She paused and Robert looked at her without speaking. Judith was 47 now and as age increases so does the probability of serious illness as a cause of unusual blood loss. If she was 20 then the odds of cancer would be minimal. Robert now had quite a few computer-based decision support aids and one of these was called QCancer and was set to encourage referral if the risk was above 3% ie a roughly 1 in 30 risk of cancer. Judith had not indicated where the blood had come from. He thought she might either be finding it difficult to find the right words to use, might be a bit embarrassed or might genuinely not be sure of where any blood has come from. Patients are often worried about what words they should use for anatomical descriptions. They are very conscious that the words they, and their friends, often use are most definitely not the ones the doctor uses! Bums, balls, bollocks, tits, boobs and arses don't feature in Medical textbooks. Patients often forget that doctors are human beings and often use these same words – probably not at work though. Incredibly some patients just don't have buttocks, testicles and breasts in their vocabulary and as, in fact, they share these features with the whole human race they then find themselves in this awkward predicament. Most simply brazen it out and Robert was more than happy with that. Some felt they had to at least try and he had experienced some unusual pronunciations of the word orifice, some patients who had got problems with their ventriculates and numerous complaints of arthuritis. Somehow it made the day more interesting he felt.

"Tell me what you have seen" asked Robert. "There's blood on the paper when I wipe after having a.............." Judith paused. Many patients would say "Shit" quite happily but this was a step too far for her. "So' you mean when you have your bowels open?" Robert helped out. He had considered adding "after you shit" but thought better of it. "Tell me about it" he encouraged with an open question. Judith described bright red blood on the paper and then told him about the gush of blood she had also seen. It left quite a few unanswered questions for Robert.

At Medical School he was taught to "clerk" a patient. Essentially this meant gathering information, weighing up its importance and generating a list of possible diagnoses in order of likelihood – a differential diagnosis list. The process was quite formulaic: you asked what was wrong (the history of the presenting complaint), followed by a number of closed questions covering the body area or system involved. Then you asked a long list of closed questions covering all the other body systems (the Review of Systems), then all about any Past Medical History, any Drugs taken or allergies, alcohol and smoking history, Family history and finally Social History(work, relationships, hobbies....) After all that you took a quick breath and examined them from top to bottom (actually top to toe – the bottom is not the bottom in this situation Robert mused). It felt like doing a 1000-piece jigsaw and collecting all the pieces one by one. It was slow, laborious and very time consuming. In retrospect he realised that this experience was a sort of programming for his mind and helped to develop an internalised sense of the relative importance of certain symptom patterns and examination findings. A bit like an apprentice carpenter he needed to try out all the tools so he knew which one to use when the time came. In his early years as a "Houseman" he had been contracted to do 90 hours per week which was probably not a very clever system but did mean he "clerked" lots of patients and gained invaluable experience.

Robert, like all experienced Clinicians, rarely consulted in this manner. He used his experience to generate a list of diagnoses often within the first few minutes. This list contained the likely diagnoses and the rarer but more serious ones that had to be considered. He then compared the patient's symptoms or "History" with these potential diagnoses to refine the list. He targeted his examination and any tests to further narrow down the possibilities and identify a way forward. Judith was 52, had 2 recent episodes of bright red rectal bleeding with some discomfort. She did not have any "Red Flag" symptoms that might suggest serious pathology like cancer (in this situation he had asked about weight loss, appetite loss, change in bowel habit and family history – someone of a young age having bowel cancer in the past could be a game-changer). His list included piles (or haemorrhoids but longer to type and more risk of spelling mistakes he thought), anal fissure and the need to discuss and exclude rectal cancer. He needed to do a PR. Not every patient's or doctor's favourite examination which is probably why it has its own abbreviation in Latin: Per Rectum. A finger in the bum. Robert's standard phrase was "At least it's over quickly".

Robert felt he had enough pieces of his jigsaw to consider the likely diagnoses. He paused. Many years ago, his progress so far might have been considered good practice. Now doctors had ICE, Helman's Model, Handing Over and a myriad of other concepts to add to the consultation. Making a diagnosis did not just involve pinning the pathology down. The concept of diagnosis now included getting a good idea of why *this* patient had come at *this* time. He needed to consider Judith's Ideas, what she was worried about (her Concerns) and what she was thinking would happen next (her Expectations). He needed to explore her health beliefs or how she thought this bleeding might be occurring, why and what it meant. He needed to give her some more time to express these ideas so they could come to an understanding and agree a way forward. Robert had been taught in an era that still saw Medicine as being "practised on patients". In many ways, patients were almost treated as passive recipients of the doctor's expertise and experience. Almost "sit down and do as you are told"! This had generally changed for the better – one of the fashionable phrases in modern practice was "sharing management options". It seemed incredible to him that this was perceived as a new concept. Robert had seen students struggling to learn how to consult like this. He'd seen many patients struggling too! The student would ask rather bluntly "What do you think is wrong?". Patients would either be frankly amazed and reply "Well you're the doctor aren't you" in a tone that definitely put the student on edge or would sort of ignore the question entirely wondering if their own ideas would perhaps sound a bit daft or frankly hilarious. In Roberts experience patients' ideas were often both! But that didn't mean they shouldn't be expressed – they were often the reason for the consultation. If Aunt Maud told them eating apple cores could damage their heart that might explain the chest pains! So, most doctors came at this question sideways. The "My friend John" technique was often used. Robert might say "I know another patient (the apocryphal John) who was worried about..." and then mention what he thought the patient might be thinking of. Even if it wasn't it would often trigger the right conversation. Many patients do not want to directly say they are worried about Multiple Sclerosis, Motor Neuron disease, Diabetes or cancer. They benefit from talking these diagnoses over with the doctor but Robert needed to find a bit of a back door to open. He found a significant number of patients did not want to use the word cancer – perhaps the modern bogeyman word. He'd seen quite a number of doctors avoid it too for the same reasons and, in his career, he had heard cancer called neoplasm, neoplastic disease, serious disease and even specific disease in situations where the patient clearly had no idea what that meant and often looked frightened.

"I do need to examine you now – is that Ok?" asked Robert. Judith nodded. Was that informed consent? Robert wondered. Every time Robert examined someone it was technically an assault. He needed to get consent for this assault – particularly if it involved the PR examination. A lot has been written on consent and it seemed a bit of a slippery subject to him. At one extreme he could explain all the ins and outs (very relevant for a PR!) of every examination, or procedure or even every drug he prescribed with all the details of why he needed to do this with every possible adverse effect and even ask patients to sign a consent form as some countries now did even for clinical examinations. On the other hand, he could skip over all this and just get on with things with little or no explanation. A lot quicker but then putting your finger in someone's bottom with no explanation might raise a few issues in the doctor-patient relationship! Finding the right balance was the challenge – and this varied from patient to patient. Robert and Judith discussed the need to examine her tummy and do a PR to exclude serious pathology. The examination was fine.

Judith got dressed and sat down again. Robert felt the consultation often seemed divided into 2 at this point. So far, he had been mostly gathering information – now it was time to work out the way forward. In the past he had been an examiner, testing student's consultation skills. He had often seen students do the information gathering excellently, listening to the patient, doing all the "ICE" stuff, encouraging, smiling and generally being all the patient could hope for. Then it came to the next stage and Jekyll-like they changed. It seemed this was the part of the consultation where they had to show how clever they were and tell the patient what was wrong and what was going to be done about it. He could often see the patient grimacing, shuffling uncomfortably in the chair and sometimes actually saying "No" to something: all cues the same doctor would have reacted to in the first part of their consultation but now all ignored. It was often at this point that the Robert had to consider the myriad of guidelines and protocols published by well-meaning bodies - the GMC, RCP, RCGP, BMA, NICE, CQC, SIGN...he could go on. These "expert" guidelines reminded him of his father's definition of the expert as "someone who knows more and more about less and less until they know everything about nothing". In fairness it always made him think that perhaps GPS "knew less and less about more and more until they knew nothing about everything". Certainly, many of these guidelines, presumably designed to make his job easier, were obscure, poorly considered for his own context, impractical and sometimes frankly obstructive. However, they carried authority and in this situation guidelines on the referral of rectal bleeding might be relevant. He had never found a guideline that included references to the patient's views. It was always "does not need referral/investigation/antibiotics" or "does need" this that or the other. Patients quite often did not want the guidelines' "does need" or vice versa.

He started discussing these points with Judith. He was aware she seemed a bit distracted particularly as he summarised her history. He paused again. "Have you got any more to add at this point?" he asked. He found it useful to "hand-over" to the patient at a number of points in the consultation. It was easy, particularly with time pressure, to motor on through but this rarely left him, or the patient satisfied. He found the challenge of doing this in his 10minutes intellectually stimulating. "Well" started Judith "I did have a similar episode of dark blood in my motion a few months ago too". Up to this point Robert had felt the likelihood of cancer was low but this changed his view. He might have discussed investigation as an option – she had described 2 recent episodes of bright red bleeding with some discomfort, she felt well, had no relevant family history and no worrying "Red Flags". These were symptoms that definitely raised alarm. Often when the patient was generally unwell with appetite or weight loss, had a long history of perhaps darker blood actually mixed with their stools, a change to looser bowels or positive findings on examination then they needed further investigation. Judith now fell into this category and warranted an urgent or "2-week referral". He needed to discuss that this was to exclude serious pathology like cancer.

Robert reflected on how much his world had changed over the years. He now lived in a world of probabilities and uncertainties. His training for this had started at Medical School. This was the era of multiple-choice questions in his examinations. Questions that contained "always" (rectal bleeding is *always* indicative of cancer) or "never" (patients under 40 with rectal bleeding *never* need referral) were always wrong and never right. Sadly, most questions contained neither and you did have to think. In the ideal world he would have figures to tell him the likelihood of each diagnosis but these figures seldom existed even nowadays. He felt patients often still saw things in black or white and did not realise how much uncertainty existed particularly for the doctor in General Practice. Statisticians to the rescue! They had provided him with "PPVs" and NPVs": positive and negative predictive values. NNTs: numbers needed to treat ie perhaps you need to treat 10 ear infections with antibiotics to cure 1 of them. Absolute and Relative Risk Reductions ARR and RRRs). He remembered the Churchillian quote about "Lies, damned lies and statistics" and over the years he had only ever found 1 patient, a retired chemist, who seemed to have a useful grasp of these concepts. He'd met many doctors who didn't too! Perhaps this was his own limitation but he felt Medicine, and patients, had quite a long way to go in this area.

Medicine is often described as an Art Robert thought. His College motto, the Royal College of General Practitioners, is Scientia Cum Caritas. Perhaps Science with caring. He felt the challenge of taking what science there was and combining it with humanity and care with the particular patient was at the heart of his job satisfaction. Patients like Judith were not aware of much of this really, but Robert knew well that they were very sensitive to Scientia Cum Caritas. Patients could spot a doctor who didn't care a mile off. Even well-educated patients had a limited appreciation in many areas. A colleague has once asked him the difference between the middle class and the lower class. Robert had declined to answer. "The Lower Class are poorly educated and poorly informed" the colleague informed him "Whereas the Middle Class are well educated and poorly informed". The internet had made matters worse really. Robert felt patients rarely saw a difference between data and information. They often looked on the web and found a lot of data from all sorts of sites. It didn't seem to matter who wrote it, what chatroom it came from or who was paying for it. They were definitely not better informed although strangely they often felt they were and this then empowered them to come out with all sorts of craziness. "Everyone should have their serum gamma-butaryl potassium hydrogenase measured – the Timbuctoo International Society of Apothecaries says so" Usually the well-educated came out with this sort of stuff and they should know better he thought.

He told Judith she should have some blood tests and be referred for a colonoscopy (more instruments in bottoms sadly). She asked if this was risky and Robert explained it did carry some risks. There were actually figures for this situation bit often there weren't. The studies that told him these figures are often carried out in a hospital setting where the patients are a selected group. They are more likely to be significantly un-well, often older and in a teaching hospital setting. Applying the results to Robert's patients might not be appropriate. The statisticians call it "Generalisabilty" (they like long words too) and generally it made Roberts life more complicated. "At least I'm not in the USA" he thought. He had seen a sign in an American shopping centre offering a free full body scan – FREE! What a bargain. Then patients forget their insides are just like their outsides. Our skins are very different, we have lumps and bumps all over the place and are positively not symmetrical. Now if you let someone scan you they are going to find things. Perhaps a cyst on your kidneys, an AVM (don't ask) in your liver, some gallstones – all of which probably don't matter at all. But know you need to see a Urologist, a Hepatologist, a surgeon. That will all cost you (or your insurance company) money and, even worse, might well involve invasive procedures. And you weren't ill in the first place! "Beware American Doctors bringing free gifts" he though - with apologies to the Trojans.

A lot of Roberts patients, politicians and even Senior Health Professionals wholeheartedly believe in the mantra "Prevention is better than cure". Difficult to argue with on the face of it but to Roberts mind a blind accept-ance of this principle led to incredibly enthusiastic endorsement of just about any screening programme an expert (remember them from earl-ier) could devise. He remembered being taught the principles needed to support a screening programme as a student. There were about a dozen or so. They included things like the disease you were trying to prevent having "a well understood development process" and a "pre-symptomatic phase" plus the treatment having "definite proven benefits over non-treatment" and the test being given to patients being well evidenced and acceptable. It seemed to him that almost none of the screening programmes met all of the points he had been taught and many were frankly ignored. But it's prevention so it must be good! A few years ago, he had attended a lecture by an American cardiologist. It was an awful lecture and he was nodding off when the lecturer put up a slide with dozens of columns and rows – exactly the sort of slide you should never put up - it was barely readable. It was a table of outcomes of surgery for heart disease. However, in the bottom left of the slide Robert noted 2 patients who had no cardiac symptoms at all who apparently had died as a result of surgery. "Aha" he thought "a mistake! He asked the lecturer to explain. Apparently, these poor patients, who had exactly NO symptoms ie they were well, had an ECG (heart tracing) which showed a slight abnormality. They went on to have invasive investigation and then surgery and then died. Be careful what you let doctors do to you Robert thought.

Robert never took the Hippocratic Oath. Most Medical Schools dropped this some years ago but it did have some interesting components. Swearing by Apollo and Aesculapius has dated a bit but "primum non nocere" or "First do no harm" seemed as relevant today as in the 5th Century BC, perhaps more so as the capacity to do harm, not just physically but perhaps financially, seems greater in modern times. He remembered research saying that 40% people stopped on a High Street have symptoms, it's part of being alive and doesn't necessarily mean you are ill. It's like the odd noises your car makes – they don't all need the mechanic.

Judith was happy to be referred – he noticed her "acceptance set". During the consultation Robert had noticed Judith's appearance and behaviour when she was agreeing with something he said. He could then sue this as a gauge to check if she was happy with what he was suggesting. In this situation Robert felt referral was indicated to rule out serious illness. Even here, he thought, patients are not generally aware of the idea of false positive and false negative investigations. They seemed to perceive medical tests as black and white too. All tests carried a risk of missing the diagnosis (the false negative) and the papers had recently described a number of cervical smears diagnosing cancer which proved incorrect (falsely positive). Patients and doctors vary in their attitude to risk. Some patients, and doctors, cannot tolerate much risk or uncertainty. They tend to want – and use - investigations and referrals more often that other doctors. Robert had come across the phrase "you get the patients you deserve" some years ago. It had a real depth of meaning – if you are good at listening, you'll get patients who talk, if you give a lot of reassurance, you'll get more anxious patients, if you are good with depression more depressed patients will see you. In this case if you refer and investigate more you will get patients who want referral and investigation. Risk and uncertainty could be the Scylla and Charybdis of the consultation. If there was little risk then a higher level of uncertainty could be tolerated - skin rashes don't usually kill so Robert could hedge his bets a bit. Chest pains can be difficult to pin down – the symptom pattern of a heart attack can be quite different in different patients. The risk might be high and the uncertainty high too. A very different challenge. Robert wondered if the corollary of the statement was "patients get the doctor they deserve"! It reminded him of the joke: "What's the definition of alcoholic? Answer: You drink more than your doctor" Perhaps patients need to choose their doctor carefully!

JIM

They married 30 years ago. An 8-year age gap seemed huge then as Judith was only 22. He swept her off her feet. She smiled. Since then the gap had narrowed. Sometimes Judith wondered if it might open up again as they got older but there was no sign of this as yet.

Jim seemed to be getting up at night 3 or 4 times recently. "It's my age" he kept saying but Judith had read a lot about prostates in the press and was worried. "Dr Roberts is about your age and you've always got on with him well" she tried to persuade, but like many men Jim was slow to make the first move. She made the appointment!

Robert saw Jim was next on the screen. He'd only seen him 2 or 3 times before – not a regular customer so his interest was stirred. "My wife thinks I need so see you about my waterworks" Jim started. Robert smiled inwardly – possibly outwardly too. Women often developed a relationship with the doctor over the years. Contraception, pregnancies and the menopause combined with the usual other complaints, plus a good set of social skills, made it easier for many women to consult their doctor. Jim had sidestepped his embarrassment by blaming Judith for the appointment! He'd then described his bladder problems with the least embarrassing worst word he could think of. Robert had a bit of work to do to help him relax a bit here.

Robert knew a few colleagues who had got into hot water with the opposite sex- and a few with the same sex too. Consultations can be quite intimate affairs – and intimate affairs have developed. They almost all ended in tears and the General Medical Council. He remembered a lecture by one of the Medical Protection Societies that all doctors have to be insured with to practice. The speaker gave some interesting advice: "If you start having sex with a patient" and everyone's interest was suddenly peaked "Don't stop! That's when the problems start." Robert thought not starting was better advice.

"Right. Tell me a bit more about your waterworks Jim" replied Robert. Jim described getting up a lot at night, and with a little prompting, a slowing of the flow and a bit of dribbling at the end. Men often describe one of "sod's" laws as "the last drip always goes down your leg" but Jim was worse than this. Robert usually asked if men could pee as high up the wall as they used to. It usually raised a laugh and an answer. It all sounded like a potential prostate issue. "Do you know much about prostate glands?" Robert asked. He expected a positive answer – the prostate gland had become a bit of a media star in recent years. "Well I have seen a bit in the press. What do you think Doc?" continued Jim. Robert was often called Doc – almost exclusively by men. He felt it was generally used to increase familiarity and perhaps bring him down to the patient's level a bit. He welcomed it.

Jim and Robert discussed prostates. Robert felt they were a bit of a design fault, perhaps like the appendix. Not particularly useful, positioned in a rather unfortunate place, and causing symptoms in 80% of 80-year olds as his old professor of surgery, who Robert noticed did urinate quite a lot, used to say. Robert got up himself 2 or 3 times a night and wondered about sharing his own symptoms with the patient. Many doctors did but he found it tended to distract from the patient's agenda. Once he told a patient he himself had a similar cyst on his scalp and, before he knew it, the patient was examining HIM! A real role reversal and best avoided he thought.

"Is there a blood test I should have?" asked Jim. "There is a test, called a PSA. Have you heard about it?" prompted Robert. The PSA test had been around almost all of Robert's career. It was a really good example of both the good and bad of medical investigations. Patients generally saw tests in black and white thought Robert. The PSA would either be positive or negative. If only that were true, he reflected. The PSA often produced false positives and negatives. It could be high and there was no cancer, or low and there was. Then there was what doctors called the "Natural History" of prostate cancer. He remembered a consultant saying men often died *with* prostate cancer and not *of* it. It was often found on post mortem examinations as a coincidental finding. It did not cause the death and the man never knew he had it. Many prostate cancers were, in the jargon, not aggressive, and would not kill. But some do. The public were generally still quite naïve in this area and believed finding a cancer was always the right thing to do. Sometimes in medicine sleeping dogs should be left alone thought Robert.

However, Jim had symptoms. The test, perhaps surprisingly, was a different test now. If you had a hundred men with symptoms the chances of the disease might, say, be 1 in 10 – 10 of them have it. If you had a hundred men with no symptoms then it might be 1% - 1 of them has it. The same test is likely to perform very differently in these 2 groups. For instance, it would be more likely to find false positives in the men with no symptoms and less likely perhaps to miss a cancer in those with symptoms. Doctors call this sensitivity and specificity. A sensitive test won't miss the cancer but will tend to suggest some cancers that aren't really there – the false positives. A specific test is good at finding those who don't have the cancer but will miss some who do – the false negatives. Using the normal level of 4 ng/ml for the PSA test its sensitivity is probably about 70%. It still misses almost a third of cancers! Its specificity is probably about 30%. So, it suggests cancer in 3 men for every real case. When you combine these figures with the fact that PSA rises with age in most men, many of the cancers are not aggressive and investigation and treatment can carry risk then the waters get very muddy indeed! This was the minefield that Jim and Robert were now in. Robert often thought about how "normal" was defined in many medical tests. The statistics used meant that normal was the range that included 95% or so of the results. So, if you had 20 tests (and that wasn't that difficult to rack up with blood tests – liver function and kidney tests together came to about 10 already) then statistically you might have at least 1 abnormal one – and there be nothing wrong! Robert had done some statistics in the past and was often shocked at the level of knowledge in this area - in himself and amongst colleagues too!

Robert took some bloods (a bit unusual for him but the examination could increase the PSA result so the bloods were best done now) examined Jim, arranged a urine test and, because he thought the prostate was a bit irregular, a review appointment to discuss all the results." Should I have mentioned my examination findings" he thought after Judith had gone. He had told him he might need further investigations and discussed those but had left it at that. The consultation had lasted 15 minutes so there was time pressure and Robert reflected that he was probably a bit "old school" here. Some might call it paternalistic or even lazy! He felt that on the basis of a rather subjective examination worrying Jim even more was not going to achieve anything more positive. Patients often felt that examination findings were black and white too, just like their tests. Robert remembered a cardiologist on a ward asking 5 of his fellow medical students and himself to listen to a patient's heart murmur. He had a stethoscope with 6 earpieces coming from the one bell you put on the patient's chest. It looked rather like a giant spider and the patient was not particularly enjoying this! All the students gave slightly different descriptions of the murmur. All except 1 who didn't hear anything! It taught Robert that examination findings could be ephemeral.

The PSA result was phoned back later that day – it was very high. Cancer was likely now.

Robert wondered if he should ask Jim to bring Judith with him. If he did then it was very likely they would work out how serious this might be. If he didn't then Jim would probably come alone and he was about to drop a bombshell on him.

Jim was feeling good. The 3 monthly injections were OK. It was 6 months since his prostate cancer was diagnosed. Now it was spring and he was tackling the garden.   Surely a bit of backache was pretty normal after gardening? It had gone on a few weeks now and was waking him at times but it would clear up – it always had in the past.

Judith made him an appointment. "I'm coming too" she said. He was a bit annoyed and felt he was being treated a bit like a child. He wasn't one for reading papers or the internet. Judith said she'd been reading about backache and was taking him to Dr Roberts.

Jim came in with Sally and sat down. Robert remembered going on a whole days training on "triadic" consultations. 3 people, or more, in the room changed things quite a bit. It was like having 2 patients at once and sometimes it was difficult to work out whom you were really treating! Why was Judith here? Jim was what doctors call a stoic. Robert remembered his ancient Roman and that stoics were conscious of the brevity of life. Unlike Shakespeare's "we strut and fret our hour upon the stage and then are gone" stoics believed in strong silent sufferance. Doctors generally respected this trait but it could be more difficult to penetrate the patient's defences to find out what was really happening.

Jim tended to be quiet at best, and monosyllabic at times Robert thought.

"How can I help?" he started. "He has some backache" Judith leapt in "I don't think it's serious" Jim replied. Robert gathered instantly what was probably going on here. Judith had probably read about prostate cancer spreading to the spine. Jim was either not aware of this possibility or using a bit of optimistic denial to cope with the anxiety. Denial was a common tool used by all humans in Robert's experience. If we are faced with a threat, a tragedy or loss we quite often try to pretend it would not, or had not, happened. It was a protection against the floods of emotion associated with these events. The challenge for the doctor was whether to work with it, go around it or go through it.

Jim described rather worrying backache. It had some of the "Red flags" doctors are told to look for. These were symptoms highly suggestive of serious pathology. Jim's pain woke him at night, he had lost a bit of weight and it was getting worse with no particular reason to do so. Robert had noticed students asking patients to rank their pain on a 1-10 scale. Robert had always seen pain as an emotion not a sensation and felt this scale a bit simplistic but apparently research had shown it had value. Jim gave it 8/10 and Robert felt this was significant. Robert needed to explain that further tests were necessary. He had a problem. Sally and Jim might well be very different in terms of how much they wanted to know and how fast they wanted to know it. His symptoms might mean the cancer had spread. Sally might ask quite specific questions about prognosis. Jim might not want to know that much.

"I think we need to do some more blood tests and a scan". Robert paused. He thought the possible link to the prostate was the proverbial elephant in the room and too big to ignore. "Did you wonder if it might be linked to your prostate cancer?" He looked intently at Jim whilst keeping an eye on Judith's reaction. He remembered being taught "questions make good statements and statements make good questions". His question was a statement – prostate cancer might be the issue here.

Jim looked down for a few seconds whilst Judith looked directly at him. He was gathering his thoughts and it was important not to interrupt him now. However, Judith rather suddenly and pointedly did interrupt. "We're not going to think about that now". She was trying to protect Jim but Robert needed to make sure this was appropriate. "Do you have any questions you want to ask me now Jim?" he asked. "Well I hope it isn't but I guess we'll have to cross that bridge if we come to it" he started. But this was only his opener and Robert's continued attention and silence prompted the next question. "What if it is the cancer spreading Doc? What happens then?" Judith had tears in her eyes now and Jim noticed. Patients often cried in the consulting room – Robert had a box of tissues strategically placed. "The blood tests and scan should tell us if that is the case and we'll get these done quickly. Then we can sort out what other treatment you might need" started Robert. But Jim was conflicted now between his role of Judith's comforter and that of a vulnerable adult. Robert recalled transactional analysis he was taught many years before. It described adopting the role of parent, child or adult in various situations often dependent on the circumstances, our previous experience and the behaviour of those around us. Jim was almost the comforting parent to Judith's child now. Sometimes patients even adopted the role of authoritarian parent in his consultations telling him off like a naughty child for something he may, or may not, have done! Now that could be interesting.

"I'm not sure if you have any more questions at this point" said Robert creating a space for Jim if he wanted it. He was already over-running a bit and he did always think of those patients in the waiting room. He had to work within the constraints of the appointment system. More time for each patient would be lovely but there were only 24 hours in a day and patient needs had to be met. A significant number of his colleagues would run 30, 40, 50 or even more minutes late routinely. The patient in the room was his main focus at that time but his own waiting time patience was only about 20 minutes and that this should be his benchmark for patients too. The doctors who did overrun often had very caring reputations but Robert felt that very long consultations should be the exception not the norm. He found the discipline of using the time he had effectively made the work both more challenging and interesting. He had been told that successful careers were often built on 3 factors. Control, Challenge and Commitment. He felt his work did involve challenge and he was committed to good care. Control was sometimes more difficult! Still 2 out of 3 aint bad he mused.

He looked at Judith and smiled sympathetically. He needed to close the consultation with her too. "Will you be coming for the next appointment?" Another question... and statement. They left together hand in hand.

Robert sighed. He always felt a bit drained after these consultations. They required focus on 2 people with possibly different agendas, their own relationship issues and different personalities. He took a slurp of coffee.

BRIAN

J im could never quite get his Dad's age right. His Dad had always been there and it felt like he would always be there too. He'd always had a cough too – after 50 years of fags who wouldn't have. But it seemed worse recently. He'd seen the advert on the TV about a cough lasting more than a month.

Robert had known Brian Davies for years. He was almost like an old friend. He liked a bit of a joke and a few pints too! He'd carried on smoking despite Robert's efforts. "I'm going to buy a hat for next time I see you" he'd said to Brian recently. Brian replied a bit confused "What the hell for?" "So, I can eat it when you give up smoking" he'd replied. But he was pretty sure his hat would be safe, sadly.

Brain came in with Jim "What can I do you for" opened Robert. One of his familiar greetings reserved for certain patients he knew very well. One or 2 even got "Oh No - not you again"! Humour was a fascinating part of his work. He sometimes thought everyone's sense of humour was unique and it could be tricky territory. Some patients treated their health with the utmost seriousness, and that was understandable and fine. A simple 1-line quip could land you in serious trouble with them. The surgery was no place for humour. Robert generally disagreed. He remembered a patient who has asked him a particularly daft question. It just so happened that one of those opaque spherical lamp shades was on the desk. He had put his hands over and it and said "the mists are clearing". He was very young at the time and the patient did not smile. He reflected that his natural inclination was of the "laughter is the best medicine" philosophy. He felt that 1 of his "internal scripts" was that life and its absurdities needed to be taken with a pinch of salt and a smile wherever possible. He had forgotten who had introduced to the ides of internal scripts but at times it did seem a useful notion. The idea that our brains, computers in many ways, are programmed during our infancy with some fixed ideas or scripts that we then carry for life. They might be "you should be kind to older people", "you should work hard" but are sometimes more negative perhaps "look out for yourself – no one can be really trusted" or "Do anything you like but don't get caught". Most people are completely unaware of these internalised drivers that impact how we relate to the world. If you become aware of them you can try and use the right script in the right place. He found out long ago that "Little old ladies are not drunks" was 1 of his own. At least twice in his career he'd been fervently trying to find out why some sweet old lady was ill only to find out it was the whisky, sherry and/or gin. He'd almost had to trip over the empties before the penny dropped.

He thought Brian had a few scripts and "doctors are busy and I shouldn't bother them" was 1 of them. Robert mused that patients seemed to fall into 2 groups. Those that came in when they didn't need to and those that didn't come when they should. Brian was the latter. "I've been coughing". Brian was not 1 to say a lot – like son like father. Robert was thinking "he's coughed for years - what's different this time?". He had to ask more direct questions than usual to get the information he needed and then he examined Brian. He was clubbed.

All Medical students are taught to start their examination of the chest at the hands – Chinese Medicine takes this to another level with a myriad of different types of pulse let alone the whole hand. But doctors look at you nails and changes to the nailbed angle and width are called clubbing. The same students are taught to regurgitate the 30 causes of clubbing but one of these is lung cancer: in an 80-year heavy life-long smoker with a worsening cough and clubbing alarm bells were ringing in Roberts mind. No patient had ever, in 35 years, come in saying their nails were changing, it appeared no one seemed to notice this.

Robert sat down. He had a multitude of thoughts in his mind. How likely is cancer? What about alternative diagnoses? I need to organise an urgent chest x ray. How much does he suspect already? What about Jim? Would Brian like to discuss this alone? How much does he want to know at this stage? How does he feel about investigations and treatment? How am I feeling about telling this old friend he might have lung cancer? Am I going to be tempted to duck the issue because I am fond of him? Robert remembered his Greek philosophy and Pandora's box. When all the other things had fled Hope was left behind – it reminded him that giving patients hope was a real kindness.

"Now Brian" started Robert with a serious tone "it's good that you are really well (start with a positive thought Robert – he'd taught may students about feedback sandwiches ie start with a good point, deliver the important information and finish with an encouraging message – it seemed appropriate here too) but I am worried about this cough and I think you need an urgent chest x ray to make sure there is nothing serious going on here". He paused. He felt he had signposted serious disease by his tone and the use of urgent and serious in the sentence. Now it was time to give Brian room to digest this and see if he wanted to pick up on these cues and ask a bit more." What do you think about this Brian?" he finished. Robert needed to see what page Brian was on here – and how many more pages he might want to turn. "I think it's the fags" Brian started, but he hadn't finished. "Could it be the big C?" Some doctors believe the likelihood of cancer should be directly discussed. They might feel Robert was sidestepping the issue somewhat. Robert felt it was kinder to lead people gently to the diagnoses rather than take them by express train! In his experience most patients were wondering about cancer anyway and it did not take long to get there.

There is a 6cm infiltrating mass in the left lower lobe of the lung. There is mediastinal widening suggestive of hilar lymphadenopathy. The appearance is highly suggestive of malignancy and an urgent referral is recommended. Robert took a breath. His worst fears for Brian were true. This chest x ray result suggested an advanced tumour which probably carried a poor prognosis. Now he had to tell Brian.

Do I phone him? Do I get him to make an urgent appointment? Should I go around to the house? He'd often said that if he turned up unannounced at a patient's house it was probably bad news. He didn't like phoning patients to give them news like this. You could see any reaction or body language and, if they were alone… well… it felt cruel. This time he was lucky – Brian was coming this afternoon. He asked a receptionist to ring Brian and ask him to come with Jim if possible.

Medical Students and Doctors are taught more than once about breaking bad news. Sometimes they learn, sometimes they don't. It's not a nice job to impart difficult life-threatening news and doctors are human. Some just need to get it over quickly and sometimes this comes across as blunt or even uncaring. Robert had run course on breaking bad news and had often used a clip from "Saving Private Ryan". In the clip the hero played by Tom Hanks is looking for a private Ryan. This soldier is the c only survivor of 4 brothers in World War II. Tom Hanks is tasked to find him and take him home. In the clip he thinks he has found Private

Ryan. He has – but it's the wrong Private Ryan and he hasn't realised. He does a lot of the breaking bad news about his brothers well but then, when he realises it's the wrong man he just leaves – and leaves the man a gibbering wreck. It was useful to get discussion going amongst the students.

Brian came in – and Jim too. Good thought Robert. "Hello Brian. Hell Jim. Come in and sit down". His tone was serious. No smile today. He was signposting. Robert remembered some research by Mehrabian that showed only 7% of meaning was conveyed by words. 38% was conveyed by what he called paralinguistics: the speed, tone and delivery of the words. More than half or 55% of the meaning was conveyed by body language. This often explained why people would say "But that's not what I said". The message they gave was not in the words. As someone had once said "Be careful what you say, it might not be what you mean".

"I need to talk to you about your chest x ray Brian. I'm afraid it's not good news". Some verbal signposting this time. Brain had avoided the word cancer last time but has referred to it. Robert felt it was the right time now. "I'm afraid your suspicions are probably right. The x ray suggests you might have a cancer". Robert paused. Brian was looking right at him but was he listening now? Patients often go numb at this point and their world contracts. They need some support and time. "Are you with me Brian?" 4 pairs of ears in the room with Jim there were useful now. "Now I am going to refer you urgently. Is that ok? For 2 reasons really: firstly, for the consultant to confirm the diagnosis and then so they can plan treatment" He stopped there. "Does that sound OK?" He remembered research showing patients often forget most of what they were told. He'd heard "Chunk. Chop, Check" as a way of increasing the chances they remember more. Sift the information into chunks. Chop them up and deliver them in these chunks. Check the patient has received them. Robert now made some space for Brian to react and gather himself together a bit. He wasn't sure how much more Brian would want to know. Some patients would have a plethora of questions at this point. For most this would take time so Robert explained this and told Brian h could ring him or see him again at any time – and Jim could do too. "Where will I go" asked Brian. Robert considered the question. In this area the answer was obvious suggesting Brian was not thinking as coherently as usual – not a surprise. He turned to Jim. He asked a few sensible questions. Robert covered a few more issues he felt were important. He remembered one of the examinations trainee GPs sat a few years ago where they were assessed by videos of consultations. They had to demonstrate "checking understanding" and almost all of them said something like "when you go home tonight what will you tell your partner about this consultation?" It often came across as rather artificial and contrived (as it was – they were doing it to pass an exam after all!) Robert had his own way of summarising for the patient. "Brian. I'm really sorry about this but I'm going to get straight onto the hospital. They will see you within 2 weeks. The consultant will want to do some tests to find out if it is cancer and this might involve the camera we've already mentioned. It might not be cancer – but if it is there will be treatment. If you are unsure about anything that is going on you are to contact me. I mean that. Have you got all that?" Brian and Jim nodded. "Now 2 other things" he continued. You will probably forget some of what we've talked about – that is natural in the circumstances. You will probably have more questions and it's my job to answer them so. Like I've said. Contact me or come and see me. And that's not just for now – it applies all though the care you'll be having. If you're not sure about something ASK. Ok?" Robert was conscious that patients often got sucked into the hospital system and he lost contact with them, even when they had worries he could help with. He wanted to be there for Brian if he was needed.

They left. Robert needed a bit of "housekeeping time" to take a breath and clear his mind for the next patient.

MOLLY

R obert knew Molly. She'd only been registered 12 months or so, worked in computer technology, had a maths degree and was anxious. She had usually read something on line or in the paper and came with a printout for him. This was not a Doctor's favourite gift.

Robert got a range of gifts from patients. There was even a sort of unspoken professional rivalry at Christmas to see how many you got! He had a patient who gave him an apple every time she came. "An apple a day keeps the doctor away "– or perhaps "at bay" in her case! His predecessor had a liking for whisky so, for many years, patients gave him bottles of Grant's or Bell's. Now 1 bottle might last Robert 10 years (although he had a weak spot for Malts and they lasted considerably shorter periods!) so he was always a good source of raffle prizes at local Fetes. He'd had a retired Art teacher as a patient. She was rather depressed and did call rather a lot. Her hallway was full of her artwork but she had put her brushes down many years before. Robert continually tried to encourage her to pick them up again. She had been a good artist and he felt this might improve her mood more than his antidepressant drugs. He was working as a locum covering maternity leave and when, after 6 months, the day to leave arrived and she asked for another visit. Robert still carried the guilt about his initial reaction of "Not again" but, when he arrived, she gave him a painting of the village. It was one of his treasured possessions. As an examiner for the General Practice exam he had asked viva questions. Candidates had to answer 6 oral questions in front of 2 examiners over 30 minutes. The questions were usually ones that had no right or wrong answer and it was more a test of attitude, and stamina, rather than facts. Most of the examiners had questions about gifts from patients. Why were they being given? What sort of gift was acceptable? When did they become unacceptable? How do you decline a gift? It was an interesting area. Nowadays GPs had to register any gifts above a certain value but when Robert phoned his local authority about this no-one seemed to have a clue what to do! Most gifts were given with a very positive intent. Rarely some were intended to manipulate and this was more difficult.

Molly had a piece of paper in her hands. His heart sank. "Heartsink" was the subject of a number of medical publications. Patients who had this effect on their doctor had been labelled rather judgementally. The "entitled demander" who paid their taxes and expected whatever drug/ treatment or referral they wanted. The "manipulative help rejecter" continually presented with a host of symptoms but had objections to most, if not all, the treatments available. The" dependent clinger" made repeated, often urgent, appointments but really just needed to see their particular doctor for reassurance – and they would be back! Finally, the "persistent non-responder" who would accept treatments offered but they never worked! Interestingly research showed that it was often the Doctors themselves who were the problem. Burnt-out, disinterested, frustrated or poorly performing doctors had more "Heart-sink" patients. The labels had, thankfully, become historical footnotes.

Patients clutching pieces of paper are not, on the whole, the doctor's favourite patients. Pieces of paper mean 1 of 3 things: They might be a list which meant time management was going to be a problem. Robert saw signs in many Practices like "The Doctor will only have time to deal with 1 problem". He always felt very uncomfortable. How did a patient know if their symptoms were related to 1 problem? Often, they came with 1 issue and the real issue only emerged during the consultation. Sometimes the second issue was truly a quick simple matter. However, his record was 10 different problems on the patient's list! That was stretching things a bit, 1 minute per problem? Did the patient really think that one through? A Practice a few years ago let patients book the time they thought they needed and it seemed to work. Robert had his doubts but was aware other research had shown patients are usually aware of the time constraint. He felt it far better to curtail the consultation if it was really lasting a long time rather than limit it from the start. Molly's paper might just be an aide-memoire and Robert, despite his antipathy for paper-carrying patients, did often encourage this. Finally, they might be media articles. From anywhere: the papers, the internet, relatives, in Turkish, Estonian or French (if he was lucky) and even from the occasional medical journal. When he was brought articles from the popular press he often wondered where patients would rather he got his expertise from: The Daily Mail or the Medical Journals?

"I've got numbness in my hands and feet and I drink too much" said Molly discreetly putting the folded A4 sheets on the desk. Robert went straight to the point. "And what do you think is wrong? What have you read?" He'd seen Molly before. She knew it and so did he. The pattern was established. She unfolded the sheets. "I think I've got diabetes". Now Molly was 35, slim and looked really well. *Whatever is the matter diabetes is well down the list* thought Robert. Robert had a personal issue with the internet. He drew a distinction between data and information. An internet search produced a flood of data on any subject. Patients could rarely sort the wheat from the chaff. They were bombarded with unregulated data and could not tell what was good data and what was not. They knew a lot more but they were not better informed. To Robert's mind information increased understanding, the internet often did not inform. It usually increased anxiety.

Robert considered his options. He remembered Michael Balint who, from the 1960s, was considered the father of modern General practice. He was not a fan of pure reassurance. He felt that doctors who used reassurance excessively increased dependence. The reassurance acted a bit like Valium. It worked but patients would become addicted and need more. He talked about doctors being like a drug. They should know when to prescribe themselves, in what dose and what the side effects might be! One of his other concepts was called "The apostolic function". This was where doctors could assume authority and proclaim the truth. It might work, it might not: not everyone is a convert! He could try telling Molly that, as an expert, he knew she did not have diabetes. Would that be enough? Robert's favourite Balint concept was "the collusion of anonymity" and most patients had experienced this. It was where patients had a problem, often not an easy one to solve, and the doctors were ducking the problem. "The consultant will sort that out", "Your GP will sort that out", "I'm only a locum". Another common ploy was the younger doctor in an outpatient clinic. They would be moving jobs in 3 months' time so could give you the next appointment in 4 months! Sometimes GPs could be thinking *he's not really my patient so I don't need to sort this out.* Robert hoped he did not fall into this trap too often.

Molly's grandmother had just developed diabetes. She'd googled the symptoms of diabetes which just about include every symptom in the book. Robert remembered a survey that showed 40% of people stopped on a street had at least some significant symptoms. Most of them were not ill.

Robert discussed that the commonest cause of her symptoms would be some worry or anxiety, directed her to a reliable, informative website she might find useful and discussed some anxiety reduction techniques. Robert considered how depression and anxiety are closely linked but Molly did not seem to have any symptoms of depression. He felt Molly saw her anxiety as outside her control. She had what doctors described as an "external locus of control". She needed someone or something to sort it out. Robert saw this as an opportunity to help her internalise this locus so she might have a bit more control over her symptoms.

"Perhaps I'm worrying about Sal". Molly paused. Robert must have looked a bit puzzled. "You know, Sally, you see her, she's pregnant". In his head there was the sound of a big penny dropping; Clang! Patients often assumed he knew the connections in their lives and often he did. But not this time. He was flooded with thoughts: *was I so distracted by Molly's anxiety and annoyed by her printouts that I did not show enough interest in her life? Am I perhaps a bit "white, male, middle class" and did not pick up on their relationship? Did they feel a bit embarrassed to tell me about their relationship and the pregnancy? Who is the father? How did they arrange this? Do the rest of the family know?* Robert felt a bit awkward – perhaps he could have made this a bit easier for Molly to bring up. "I'm sorry" an apology. Robert felt sorry a rather underused word, "I didn't realise Sally was your partner".

Molly then described her anxieties about having a family and the effects of their own relationship dynamics. This was the first time Robert had really talked *with* her. He felt he had talked *to* her a bit too much perhaps. He reflected how a number of patients "tried out" a doctor, perhaps consciously but often subconsciously, before they trusted them enough to talk about the real issue. Sadly, it was often some sort of abuse. Gladly not so this time.

Molly left. In retrospect Robert realised he had always felt a bit disappointed after her previous consultations. Now he had mixed feelings. Had he been a bit slow in building their relationship? This consultation seemed like a big step forward - for both of them. It was certainly a learning experience for him. He was reminded of the story of the oracle at Delphi. In the ancient Greek world there was a crack in the rocks and the priestess could inhale the vapours from the fissure and, in a state of trance, answer any question you had. The answers were notoriously ambiguous. However, written above the door, importantly before you entered, was the phrase "Know thyself". The message was clear: if you understood your own nature and situation why are you entering here? Robert felt both Molly and he now knew themselves a bit better. It also reminded him of the Cycle of Change. Patients might be ready to change their behaviour, they might just be thinking about it, or they might not even know a change would be beneficial. This model encouraged him to think about how he could move patients around in the right direction. Perhaps both Molly and he had moved a bit today as well.

After the surgery he went to deal with his in-tray. There was an article from the Daily Mail that a patient had helpfully left him, with good intent at least. It said that a particular chemical reduced the incidence of heart disease by 40% and could save thousands of lives. He grinned. He'd only ever met one patient who understood the difference between ARR and RRR. Absolute Reduction Rates and Relative Reduction Rates. When he found the original paper on-line, he found that this drug reduced the chances of a heart attack from 5 in a thousand to 3 in a thousand. He would have to explain that 1000 patients would need to take the drug for at least 5 years to stop 2 heart attacks. The RRR was 0.2% ie 2 in a 1000. The ARR was from 5 to 3 cases - the 40% the paper mentioned. Now the drug was actually just a newer version of an established drug and it cost more. It was one of the usual tricks the drug industry employed to advertise their products. Then the article said it would save thousands of lives. *Wonderful* thought Robert *It's the elixir of life, we'll all live forever*. Sadly, we all die of something and no drug ultimately saves lives he mused.

Patients were usually unaware of NICE (the National Institute of Clinical Excellence), one of the many bodies of experts that regularly sent Robert guidelines telling him how to practise. He thought NICE did not have a particularly nice job: getting experts to agree was not an easy task. He felt patients would be surprised, perhaps even horrified, if they knew how little evidence there was on some pretty crucial areas of Robert's work. He remembered being taught about "the hierarchy of evidence". The best evidence about which treatments to use would come from tests that were double-blind, randomised, controlled trials. This meant that neither the doctors nor the patients in the trial knew who was taking the active treatment. The patients were selected at random for the treatment and only after the trial finished did everyone get to know which group they had been in. These sorts of trials were fairly rare. What Robert also remembered was that expert opinion was well down the list in the hierarchy – almost at the bottom really. Sadly, guidelines were often based on expert opinion. "Experts again" he mused. NICE often used QALYs. The Quality Adjusted Life Year was an attempt to quantify the benefit of a treatment in terms of how much good life it gave the patient. 1 QALY was a year of perfect health and was a sort of statistical manipulation for health economists but was now used to justify funding decisions. It was fraught with difficulties, particularly for treatments in the elderly whose life expectancy was shorter so treatments attracted less QALYs. Now if a drug costs £10,000 and extends life by 6 months it costs £20,000 per QALY. Robert was aware that NICE used £20-30,000 per QALY as their cut off. Above this treatment on the NHS might be restricted. It was a difficult area. Rationing was a bit of a dirty word in the NHS, often unspoken and not discussed. Increasingly General Practice has been subjected to targets and restrictions as budgets were tightened. He wondered about the morality of actively trying to reduce referrals to save money. He worried about the drive to treat more patients with less money available. He worried about how all this was portrayed in the press and how Medical Students were turning their back on his branch of the profession as they perceived it as an over-regulated medical treadmill.

Robert typed his note on Molly's file. His typing skills were pre-historic and his IT skills a little better. He remembered the days of written notes and even the days when patients did not have access to their notes. One colleague had vented his frustration and written, across the whole A4 page, in large and emotive style "On No! Not again!". The patient was well known. It was probably still there.

JIM

J im's symptoms were much better on the 3 monthly injections and life was pretty much unchanged. He had been frightened by the backache but the scan had come back as normal - well that's how Dr Roberts described it. Doctors used the words "wear and tear" reassuringly although he was not so sure how "worn and torn" he really wanted to be! But it was not the cancer so a bit of backache was OK by him. Looking back, he realised he'd learnt a lot about the medical profession and particularly about what they termed "management". Dr Roberts had primed him for this right from the beginning. "You'll probably be given a number of options about your treatment" Robert had said "And a lot of information verbal and written: it can be a bit overwhelming so take your time and think about it when you are ready". He was right. He had somehow thought he would be prescribed a treat-ment and told all about it. He discovered that there were at least 3 options and then almost asked to choose which one he wanted. Thankfully Judith had come with him and asked the sensible questions he couldn't think of at the time.

There were some side effects though and he decided to see Dr Roberts. He didn't say anything to Judith. Robert saw Jim's name on his appointment list. He hadn't seen much of him since the prostate cancer was diagnosed. Once treatment had started patients seemed to drift off into the hospital system and he often wondered how they felt about this. Would they still like to see him occasionally to discuss things? Or not? How often? Should he try and contact them a bit more? Would that be welcomed? Or not? Some patients did come quite regularly, some hardly at all. He tried to make them know he was available. Was that enough?

Robert thought Jim looked well as he entered, that was a good start he thought. "How are you doing?" he started. There was a pause which told Robert this was perhaps not quite as straightforward as it might have been. "I've got some swelling" Jim said a bit hesitantly. He was signposting his problem in exactly the same way Robert did for difficult, or embarrassing problems. Robert knew what treatment Jim was on. He had an inkling he knew where this swelling was. Could he make it easier for Jim? "Are we talking about chest swelling?" he replied. Jim looked relieved. "It's my treatment I think and I can't stop that can I?" he continued. "let's have a look" said Robert.

Jim had pretty mild gynaecomastia. Robert laughed at the way the Macmillan website helped people to say it: guy-nee-co-mass-tee-ah. He was a bit ashamed at the amusement he, and his colleagues, derived from patients' pronunciation of medical terms. Heart attacks were often coronararies, sore joints were arthuritis (poor Arthur!) and one patient with Jim's problems told everyone he had apostate cancer! Over the years various medical secretaries had typed mistakes that made the letters much more interesting than the correct terminology. The most amusing example was a handwritten letter by one of his trainees. He had admitted a 51-year old farmer and, in his slightly scrawled handwriting, had started the letter "This 51y old farmer...." It looked exactly like he had written "This Sly old farmer...." The patient had read the letter and was not impressed.

Jim put his shirt back on and sat down. Robert washed his hands and sat too. He explained that Jim was right, this was a common side effect of the treatment. He asked how it was affecting him, particularly whether it was an issue in his relationship. Jim might be reluctant to raise this himself. Jim's major concern was how big his new breasts might become!

When Robert qualified the world was a different place. Doctors generally did prescribe a treatment, the one they felt was the best. Patients generally listened and accepted this. Whether they took the treatment was another thing. In those days the word for this was compliance. By inference patients were expected to be compliant with all its undertones of bending to the doctor's will. These days the word had changed. Now it was concordance, with its undertones of working together. All the research showed that this increased the number of patients who actually completed the, agreed, treatment plan. The jargon for how to achieve this was "sharing management options". This encouraged the doctor to put all the possible options on the table, explain what they all meant, and act as a sort of mentor to help the patient decide. Now Robert had noticed that people varied in how much they wanted to "share management options". Patients and Doctors alike. One A&E doctor had no time for it at all. Robert could see his point to a degree. If you were having a stroke you needed treatment now. However, in most situations, it was a blindingly obvious good idea that it had only taken the medical profession hundreds of years to recognise! But, thankfully (or life would be very dull Robert often thought) patients varied too. Some really did not want to "share management options" and just wanted "the best" treatment. The most difficult patients were those that, similarly, did not want to share management options, but wanted possibly the worst treatment: at least from the medical point of view. They often had negative experiences of conventional medicine, were aware they needed some sort of treatment and determined to avoid the obviously best approach. They reminded Robert of a book he read "Games people play". It described some of the patterns of behaviour people adopt and one of these games was "that won't work". Every time the doctor suggests a solution, often wracking their brains to try and find a way through the impasse, the patient replies with a reason why that won't work. It becomes like an endless tennis rally with the ball going forward and backwards between patient and doctor with no end in sight. The solution for the doctor is to stop hitting the ball ie stop suggesting a solution and get the patient to define the way out. Often harder than it sounds.

Jim was not playing games. Robert described his options. Including the one doctors sometimes miss – doing nothing. Robert had always liked what were termed "Consultation" models. They were ways of understanding the progress of a consultation and there were a lot of them. Helman's model was one of his favourites. It encouraged the doctor to think about the patient's perspective. It postulated that the patient had a number of questions in mind. What has happened? Why has it happened? Why has it happened to me? Why has it happened now? What would happen if nothing were done? What should I do? What can you do? Robert remembered doing a "Learning style" assessment many years ago. This particular exercise divided people into 4 groups: Activists who like to learn by doing, Reflectors who need time to digest and learn, Pragmatists who want to learn how and now and Theorists who like to understand the basis for the learning. He had discovered we are all mixtures of these categories but do tend to fall into certain combinations. He had made the assumption that doctors would all be similar: he was wrong. His own tendency was quite strongly theorist and this was not shared by many of his colleagues who found theory, and models, amusing enough but not very useful for them.

Jim wasn't too bothered about doing anything right now although Robert did discuss the various options. They finished discussing exogenous oestrogens, that Jim might reduce his exposure to, and agreed to review the problem in a few months. Robert did direct him to the Macmillan website.

"How is your father doing?" Robert asked as Jim was getting ready to leave. One of the most rewarding aspects of being a GP, a Family Doctor Robert thought, was getting to know a whole family. Robert treated 4 generations of some families and he often felt that illness behaviour ran in families. He had attended a course on "family scripts" as part of a Narrative Medicine Programme. He'd learnt how we all like to tell stories that are coloured by our experiences, society, relationships and culture, and that this is part of how we all make sense of existence. Many of the thought processes are conditioned by our childhood. He was reminded of the book "Families and how to survive them" published by John Cleese and his therapist many years before this course. We are "programmed" in many ways by our upbringing and share patterns of thought and behaviour (or scripts like in a play) with our relations. The Family Doctor sees these scripts in action and can try to play his part in the family life in an appropriate way. It was a real privilege.

"He's struggling" Jim said sombrely. This family had always had the script of minimising medical issues. Brian was much worse or Jim would have said nothing. "I need to see him" replied Robert "Could he come in or do I need to visit?". "I'll bring him in" said Jim.

MOSES

Robert had been a GP trainer for some years. The budding GPs had already been qualified for 2 or 3 years before they came to the practice for what was a sort of apprentice year. It seemed ironic to him that it took 10 years to train as a GP of which only about 18 months was actually spent in General Practice. The power base of Medical Education had always been the University Hospitals and it was only recently that the importance of experience in the community had been recognised.

Moses had a West African background. Like many overseas Doctors he had decided to use his, very Christian, name and was Dr Moses. His African surname appeared on official paperwork but Robert never heard it used. Moses had done his undergraduate degree in Africa but made his home here. Robert reflected the UK had never had any moral doubts about attracting Staff from impoverished third world countries while UK trained Doctors were leaving for better working conditions abroad. Coupled with the fact that the politicians had ignored the evidence that we needed to train more Doctors in this country it meant the NHS relied on these Doctors to keep going.

When Moses started in the Practice, he was a fairly typical trainee, or Registrar as they were now termed. After years of hospital experience these doctors were used to ill patients – often very ill patients. In the context of the hospital a chest pain has very different significance to the chest pain in the GP surgery. In the hospital it was much more likely to be serious illness, perhaps cardiac, than in the GP setting where a more benign cause was more likely. The GP needs to identify the serious problems amongst the sea of relatively minor illness, in 10 minutes. The Registrars are not expected to do this immediately and are usually given 20- or 30-minute appointments at the start. Patients often quite like these appointments. They are more likely to be examined, more likely to be investigated and more likely to be referred and many like this perceived thoroughness. The Registrars have more time to talk and Moses, with his quiet, thoughtful approach was a good listener. One of the greatest compliments Robert thought a GP could receive was "Thank you for listening to me". Registrars were used to working as part of a team. Patients in hospital usually saw nurses, physios and other doctors. In the Practice patients just saw them, and no -one else. They came in and went out and this left many Registrars worried about all the potential "what ifs". They had to adjust to this anxiety and learn to "safety net" the consultation. Moses adjusted well.   He developed quite a following with patients and staff alike.

Over recent years Robert thought GP training had undergone a paradigm shift. As the concepts of trust and professionalism were being redefined by a society that was becoming more informed and more questioning there was a call to make training more accountable: the e-portfolio of competencies was introduced. Registrars had to collect and record evidence that they were competent in a vast array of areas. Robert saw it as the Hydra: a many-headed monster that constantly needed feeding. A beast of a thing, and many Registrars shared his view. For the vast majority of them it became a mechanistic time-consuming and frustrating chore. Robert recalled 2 metaphors for education. The e-port-folio was like a building. You put it together according to a plan, brick by brick to create a solid, defined, measurable design. Robert preferred the gardening metaphor: you planted seeds, watered and nurtured them, pruned if necessary and let the Doctor grow. The e-portfolio produced trained GPs. Robert preferred educated ones. If you teach people how to learn then you don't need to teach them anymore, he thought.

Almost all GPs are taught about how people learn. The one model that amused Robert concerned competence. Registrars started with "unconscious incompetence". They didn't know what they needed to know! They all needed close supervision at this stage. Then they had an experience that made them aware of a deficiency – perhaps a rash they didn't have a clue about. This was "conscious incompetence". The next stage was "conscious competence" where they could do the job but needed to concentrate quite hard on what they were doing. Finally, Practitioners reach "unconscious competence". They do the work well but if you asked them how they would struggle to tell you. Robert always thought of adults riding a bike here – if you asked most of them how they did it they would just say "get on and pedal". They had forgotten how they learnt to balance this unstable contraption. According to one of his theorist Registrars it was all "social science crap". Robert found these ideas useful at times though.

Robert went into Moses' room 1 day about a month after he arrived. The notice board was covered with at least 30 bright yellow post-its. It reminded Robert of a scene from the film Bruce Almighty where Jim Carrey's character was trying to answer all of God's prayer list and had the prayers converted into post-its that then covered everywhere! Moses was not in that state but this was clearly a system that would not last and he hadn't considered what patients might make of his yellow snow storm! They discussed other ways of recording things he needed to remember – he changed his system. Registrars are expected to demonstrate the knowledge, skills and attitudes that would make them a competent GP. In practical terms this means learning to think, learning to do and learning to care and cope. The idea of learning to care had always seemed a bit strange to Robert but many Registrars did need to learn how and when to express sympathy, perhaps empathy and definitely when caring involved confronting the patient to a degree. Robert had 1 Registrar who was particularly grumpy. He ignored this for a-while but both staff and patients were making comments so he felt he had to act. When he approached the Doctor, he was surprised to learn he believed that if you were nice to people they would abuse you. This had its roots in a boarding school upbringing. Robert suggested this might be a false belief and wondered if they might test it out. They agreed the Registrar would be actively pleasant to 2 members of staff perhaps with just a cheery good morning. At the time it all felt a bit puerile but within a week the staff were asking what he'd done to the Registrar! He was even seen smiling! Such Damascene conversions were rare though. Most Registrars were young, enthusiastic and a joy to help.

Moses passed his exams and stayed in the NHS.

BRIAN

Brian came with Jim a week later. Robert noticed it took much longer for them to get to his door than their usual few seconds. Brian looked pale, he'd lost weight and was out of breath. He smiled at Robert.

Robert was aware of the roller coaster ride patients experienced with the diagnosis of cancer. It started with the devastation of the news and then improved as some treatment was offered. The treatment then often made things worse again, sometimes patients even felt worse than when they were first diagnosed at this stage. Then they improved and spirits rose. Too often remission was followed by relapse. Brian was at this point.

"Struggling a bit?" asked Robert. "You noticed" Brian smiled weakly. Brian's disease had spread. Robert needed to assess how much his symptoms could be improved and how. That was going to mean more blood tests and scans. How was he coping at home? What help did he want? What help did he need? These 2 things were often different and Robert often had to help people to accept the help they needed, particularly with the stoic families. He wanted to introduce the idea of seeing the Macmillan Nurse for more help and support. These Specialist Nurses were invaluable to both him and the patient, he reflected. Patients had their own ideas about these Nurses often believing they were there for the terminal period only and introducing the idea of seeing them could sometimes be tricky.

Within the week Brian had had his investigations. They showed an extension of his cancer with liver involvement. Most patients understood the concept of secondary spread of a tumour to other areas of the body and many realised liver spread was a sinister development. Robert went around to see him at home. He had been taught the value of seeing patients at home as a student. You usually had a bit more time (not much more sadly he thought as he drove over to Brian's house on a local estate), patients were usually pleased to see you and more relaxed in their own environment. He was taught to assess the home in terms of its access, cleanliness, self-caring facilities and even what it told him about the patient in many others ways. What pictures were on the walls? Was it warm? What books were there around? (often indicative of educational level and understanding). What evidence was there of social support? The list could go on he thought. When he started Practice some years before home visits were common. There had been a steady erosion of this sort of practice. The visit usually took at least twice and sometimes far longer than an appointment. There was a limit to what could be done, even in terms of examination, in the home setting and some doctors felt vulnerable on their own. Sadly assaults, never even mentioned in his undergraduate course, were a regular event in the NHS of today. Some GPs did perhaps 2 or 3 visits a week. In his own Practice, clinging to what some might call outdated values, GPs did about that number per day. He was proud of this but wondered how long it could continue. Patients had consulted him by phone for years and he had run courses on remote consultation skills, teaching colleagues the limitations of consulting without visual cues and feedback. It was now an accepted form of "seeing" patients whereas he remembered a letter in the British Medical Journal in the 1990s from a senior doctor who thought anyone assessing a patient over the phone was negligent! Many Practices had responded to overwhelming demand by introducing "telephone triage". The word triage derives from the French "to sort". The idea is to sort out who can be dealt with over the phone, who needs to be seen and the urgency issues involved. Doctors can take a-while to adjust to new ways of working. Robert reflected on how conservative the profession had been over hundreds of years. Refusing to accept Lister's ideas on germ theory, Jenner's ideas on vaccination, the concept of anaesthesia... the list could go on and was probably being added to in each era. Patients needed time to adjust too and generally they don't like phone consultations, that is unless they do! Some fairly straightforward issues can be dealt with over the phone, others cannot. His own Practice had found that making all patients phone actually added time to the day's work! He felt it encouraged some bad habits too: giving out antibiotics a bit too easily, taking risks with some problems when an examination was probably wise and, when faced with perhaps 30 calls to make, cutting dangerous corners. His mind re-focused, somehow the car seemed to have decided to stop: he was in Brian's drive.

Brian was alone today and was warm, well supplied and Judith was coming around later. They sat together. "Do you want some tea?" Brian asked. This was a common offer and kindly meant but tea is hot and takes quite a long time to drink. Robert declined. "How are you managing?" Robert started. Brian was managing and the Macmillan Nurse had been round and seen the family together. "I need to talk to you about the test results" Robert signposted. Brian looked directly at him, a bit more in resignation than in hope "It's not good is it Doc?" he stated. "The tumour has spread I'm afraid" Robert paused allowing that to sink in a bit "but we can still help you feel better than you do now Brian" he continued. Brian averted his gaze. Patients often cried in front of him and that was fine but Brian was not that sort of character. Robert suspected any tears he had would come with family. There was silence for a time. Robert had needed to learn how to tolerate this. "Nature abhors a vacuum" he always thought and most people can't tolerate silence for long. But at times it is the best way to let the patient have the time they need. Brian looked up. "Have you got any more questions at the moment?" asked Robert. Brian had very little more to ask at this point. Robert reflected how modern medicine generally gave patients a lot of information. The test findings in detail, side effects, piles of written information, prognosis and all the sources of help. It was now the way of the world but he had his own doubts. Sometimes he thought patients should lead the process a bit more, perhaps getting the information at the rate they needed or wanted? Was this another example of him going past his own sell-by date!

Robert worked in what was termed "Primary Care ". This involved the team of people – the Primary Care Team – all the health care workers who saw the patients as a point of first contact. When he started Practice it meant him, a part time Practice Nurse, a health visitor and a district nurse. Now there were GPs, Practice Nurses, Nurse Practitioners, Health Visitors, Phlebotomists, Counsellors, District Nurses, Health Care Assistants, Primary Care Mental Health Workers, Midwives, Social workers, Macmillan Nurses, Community Specialist nurses, Physician assistants, Pharmacy Assistants...no wonder patients were a bit confused. He certainly was! Now there was increasing call for email contact, skype consultations, health text-messaging and even artificial intelligence physician support. In years gone by, perhaps 15 years ago he thought, you felt you might be able to predict what the Primary Care landscape might look like and certainly felt the Family Doctor had a place in it. Recently he had read about the demise of the Family Doctor with some academics even suggesting that the model of care he had provided, and valued all his life,

was not fit for purpose in the 21st century. Interestingly these articles did not seem to consider what patients felt about these developments. Robert had always wondered about what doctors termed continuity of care.

In the latter half of the 20th century GPs were on call almost 24/7. They had few holidays, covered the nights and worked long days. He thought these Doctors might laugh at the modern concept of continuity but he also knew many patients who valued knowing and seeing the same doctor over years. If this changed we will all be the poorer, he thought.

TARA

Tara was 6 months old, born in April. Robert thought Spring was a good time to have a baby. Six months of growth before the next round of winter viruses arrived seemed a good start. Now extended families living close together were rare, parents often shouldered the burden of children alone. Most people had never seen a really ill child and these factors generated anxiety. "The average 0-5-year-old child gets 6-9 infections per year" his professor of paediatrics had told him. That was the average; some lucky child was getting 1 or 2, and another not so lucky a dozen or more. If these were mostly winter bugs then that was 2 a month. Enough to cause any parent anxiety.

Tara came in, with Molly and Sally. Both parents coming with a child usually meant something. Possibly a whole lot of somethings. Very caring parents, both being at home on the day, only 1 driver in the family and, quite often, an indication of shared anxiety. The parents felt they both needed to be there to provide mutual support and to make sure their anxiety was communicated; essentially that they were listened to. "She's been so ill for a week" Molly started, "and she's got a rash" Sarah interjected urgently.

GP training involves 5 years at Medical School, 2 years as a junior doctor and then 3 more years as a GP Registrar. In the last 3 years about 18 months will be spent in a GP Practice as a sort of apprentice. The mechanics of the process involve choices. Not every GP is able to do a post in paediatrics. Surprisingly some GPs go through all their training with little experience of some specialities: dermatology, ENT and ophthalmology being prime examples. Robert had done paediatrics in a London teaching hospital, perhaps not the best setting for a career as a GP, but he had learnt one major lesson – how to spot an ill child. It might sound easier than it is but children can get ill very quickly. Thankfully they are equally good at recovering too. Seeing an ill child was an almost visceral experience: you felt it in your gut. They were often quiet, pale, inactive and "easy" to examine. If you held them in your arms, they felt leaden. It almost made you shudder. Most GPs spot these children as they enter the consulting room. Thankfully Tara did not seem to be in this state.

Robert knew that the UK's record of dealing with seriously ill children did not compare well with other European countries. In many of these countries family doctors did not see children at all. Children saw paediatricians who worked in the community. In an ideal world all GPs would get paediatric training he thought. In recent years a "Traffic light" system had been introduced to try and improve the early recognition of the ill child. Basically, it consisted of a number of symptoms and signs that placed the child in Green, Amber or Red categories. It encouraged GPs to measure the pulse rate, respiratory rate, temperature and capillary refill time (CRT) of all young infants with a fever. The CRT was a measure of how quickly skin colour returned after light pressure and was not a sign Robert had been taught about as a student. Medical science moves quickly and quite a lot of what he had been taught was now out of date or just simply wrong. As a student he would have failed a question about the treatment of heart failure if he had suggested using the drugs called Beta-blockers. Now he would fail if he didn't mention them! Over his career there had been all sorts of systems to try and encourage GPs to keep up to date. Currently he was expected to do at least 50 hours of Continuing Professional Development (CPD) and then have a satisfactory annual appraisal. This consisted of documenting his CPD, what difference it had made to his practice, provide some evidence for changes in his practice and then meeting for about 2-3 hours with an appointed colleague to go over this. Every 5 years a Regionally appointed senior doctor would review these appraisals and hopefully sign him off as "Validated" or "Revalidated" as it was usually termed.

Tara was "Green". Molly and Sally had been googling again and found meningitis. Bacterial meningitis terrified Robert almost as much as it terrified parents, perhaps even more so. It could overwhelm in hours without giving much of a clue that it was brewing. Every year the press contained stories of the Casualty Officer or GP who sent a child home who was dead with this monster of a disease within hours. Molly had done the glass test on Tara's rash. She had pushed rather gently and the rash had not faded. Robert explained how the test was designed to see if the rash would "blanch". He then used his finger to push on the rash and released the pressure. The rash faded and reappeared. They discussed viral illnesses, meningitis and even Traffic lights (Sally had found this on the net too!). "She's teething too" said Sally as the consultation seemed to be ending, a common time to bring up a whole new problem as if it would be a quick and easy issue for him to solve. This might be, but sometimes patients, after 10 minutes or more had gone by, would announce "... and I have been having chest pains". Not quick and easy and not ignorable either! "Are there any homeopathic remedies we might use?" she continued. Robert had been using chamomile granules for years. They were small round balls that babies could roll around their gums. How they worked he had no idea but they were cheap, with no side effects and, according to many parents, highly effective. There was now a move to stop all homeopathic prescriptions on the NHS based on their being no current scientific understanding of their mode of action or evidence of their efficacy. It made Robert think of the ethical bases of his work. Patients were encouraged to be autonomous: to make their own decisions. This gave him a duty to inform them as best he could to try achieve an informed decision. This was sometimes termed informed consent. Robert often wondered how informed this consent actually was. In an ideal world a patient, with some ability to understand, might listen to all the pros and cons and the doctor's view, and then have time to reflect and make a decision that would then be discussed together to form a way forward. In reality this rarely happened. Even the Courts had decided Doctors did not have to mention serious complication with a <1% occurrence rate. In a 10-minute consultation inevitably quite a lot was left unsaid. Robert had a duty to do some good, rather obvious he thought, coupled with the duty to do no harm; much more difficult "primum non nocere" or First do no harm seemed as relevant today as it did more than 2000 years ago. As relevant but perhaps more problematic. Modern medicines and surgery carried more risk of serious adverse effects than in previous centuries perhaps. Justice was the final component of this ethical model. Moral justice meant being open and honest with patients. When Robert first qualified Doctors often, perhaps at the request of well-meaning relatives, concealed a malignant diagnosis. This was thankfully rare these days. Social justice placed a pressure on Robert to use NHS resources wisely and fairly. Perhaps raising the thorny issue of rationing. Finally, legal justice covered the various laws that applied to his work. Acts like the Mental Health Act, The Mental Capacity Act and the Children's Act were well known by most GPs. The latter decreed that Robert must have the child's best interests at heart. Usually that concurred with the parental interests. The press often documented the tragic cases that could occur and be complicated by a difference between legal, parental and professional opinions. In his own world the occasional cases of child abuse where he had a duty to involve Child Protection teams were the most challenging and distressing.

More recently the Mental Capacity Act had been passed. It was heralded as the most sensible piece of Medical law ever passed. Basically, it translated everyday good practice into law. Some patients with an impairment of brain function found it difficult to make decisions for themselves. The law ensured Robert judged that the patient was able to take in and consider the relevant information and then make a decision. They were allowed to make a bad decision but only if they could demonstrate understanding! If they could not meet these criteria then Robert could act in their best interests with the least restrictive measures. Robert had allowed the staff of a nursing home to hide life-maintaining medicines in food for a patient with dementia on this basis.

Sally asked for some calpol for Tara. Prescribing, and prescribing costs, were a major pressure in Robert's practice. The NHS drug bill had mushroomed over the years and the local authority kept this under review. Practices were offered incentives to stick to budget. Robert wondered about the ethics of asking him to reduce his prescribing particularly when it went hand in hand with a pressure from the same authority to prescribe more medicines to control other diseases, like diabetes or high blood pressure. Calpol was not actually prescriptible, some medicines were black-listed, but paracetamol syrup was. Branded drugs with trade names were often more expensive so the generic, or scientific-named medicine was recommended. Paracetamol was also purchasable from the chemist. Should Robert be nice and prescribe the paracetamol? Most GPs like to be liked. So did he.

Patients offered struggled with the "needs versus wants" dilemma. Robert offered what he thought they needed. They might ask for what they wanted. Sometimes the 2 did not correspond. Robert had been taught NESCAFE to help his prescribing. Was the drug Necessary? Was it Effective, Safe and Cost-effective? What Alternatives are there? What Follow up is necessary and does the drug have any unusual Extra features? Some patients were very particular about their medicines. Most tablets are made of the relevant drug plus a number of other compounds. These are fillers, stabilisers or adjuvants that help the active component work. Patients were sometimes sensitive to some of these components and it could be very difficult to find alternatives. Often the evidence that this component was causing the side effect the patient described was difficult to prove and it could result in a bit of a difficult consultation, particularly if the alternative was a "special". Specials were medicines mixed specifically for that patient and could be ridiculously expensive – sometimes thousands of pounds. The local Authority took a particular interest in them and Robert's life could prove very interesting unless he had very good grounds to use them!

GPs had very mixed feelings about allergic reactions. Robert felt allergy was generally poorly understood and certainly poorly taught. Many patients were convinced they were allergic to various compounds even when medically there was little evidence of definitive allergic reactions. Medically they were "intolerant" of the compound in question. In practical terms it was very difficult, if not impossible, to test a reaction to the thing in question and it all seemed a bit academic

anyway. If a patient felt something was causing intolerable symptoms they were not going to take it again, were they? Robert felt it best to work with them. He had seen colleagues directly challenge these beliefs with patients and the relationship became, at best strained, more usually it broke down completely. The history of Medicine seemed to him to be full of examples of doctors believing they knew better (cupping, blood-letting, arsenic were all examples) only for time to expose their ignorance. He felt some of this was still happening today. He once heard a consultant say that only half of what he was practising was effective. The only problem was he didn't know which half! Sadly, that consultant's humility was often not shared by other Doctors.

Molly, Sally and Tara left. Tara smiled at him. He smiled back.

BRIAN

B rian was dying. Robert had seen him deteriorate in recent weeks and he was now bedbound in his living room. It was a painful process to watch the strength ebbing from him and Robert could only imagine how this might feel to his family. He wondered whether Brian would develop "the old man's friend". This was a chest infection or bronchopneumonia that was considered, by doctors, to be a kinder death. The District Nurses were visiting daily and the family had arranged a rota of care. It was heartening to see a family pull together in the face of certain tragedy.

Thankfully weakness was Brian's only real symptom. Thankfully because pain and other symptoms would have required more medication. Less thankfully because Robert felt hopeless to relieve the fatigue. He wondered about talking to Brian about his beliefs around death and dying. He realised he lived in an increasingly irreligious society but, to his mind, lack of religious belief did not mean lack of spirituality. He'd had many difficult, and rewarding, discussions with dying patients about what they believed and how this affected their approach to this particular door. Sometimes patients, who had never attended a church, or a mosque, would like to talk to the priest or Imam. It helped to know these people as it needed to be handled with respect and kindness rather than fervour: not all priests or Imams were the same. These discussions had become less common over the years too, he felt. The "Extended Primary Health Care Team" had taken over many of the parts he had played in patients' lives. Sometimes he missed these roles.

Brian died at 6am on a Friday morning. Robert had left his home number for Jim to call as he expected the death that night. He had completed the "DNAR" form a few days earlier. Sometimes the family, quite understandably, panic as death approaches and call 999. Sadly, some patients are then taken to hospital when that is the last thing they wanted. In recent years the DNAR – Do Not Attempt Resuscitation – form emerged as a solution to this. The form is completed and signed and left at the house. The family and patient are aware of this. The timing for its completion can be an issue. Robert considered how the idea of "tick-box" medicine had evolved in recent years. If A is happening then B,C,D,E...are necessary. It could become a bit mechanical or robotic and patients asked about whether they wanted to be resuscitated at a time when they were still adjusting to the idea of a terminal illness existing at all. Clinical judgement and knowing your patient were vital here Robert believed.

Brian wanted to be cremated. Robert had to see the body and he did this at the local undertaker. He wrote a death certificate which had to be issued by a doctor who knew the patient and had ideally seen them in the 2 weeks prior to death. A second doctor from another Practice had to sign the cremation form as well so Robert needed to ring a local colleague and explain the circumstances. This doctor would usually contact the family so he explained this to Jim. Some families could be very upset by the processes around death, particularly sudden death. If he, as the GP, could not issue a death certificate for these cases, perhaps the patient had not been seen for some time and death was unexpected, then the Coroner had to be informed. This meant that a Policeman would visit to ascertain any suspicious circumstances. It meant that the Coroner's undertaker would be involved. It might mean a post-mortem examination was ordered. When a family is plunged into sudden grief these things can add to their distress.

Robert tried to explain the likely effects of grief to the family. These stages had been described many years ago and were a basic human reaction to loss. Often denial cut in first. This hasn't happened. This can't happen. Very understandable and it probably explained why patients often saw, heard and talked to lost loved ones. Anger of some sort is usually present and could take various forms. A wife might fume at her husband for leaving her behind. Worse still she might direct her anger inward at herself tearing at her own soul in her distress for some perceived error or action with regret. Families would squabble at best, at worst stop talking to each other. The anger might be directed at Robert or the Hospital, or just generally the medical profession for letting the patient down. Sometimes this was justified. Care is seldom perfect and sometimes far from it. Sometimes this anger persisted and seemed to take the grief process over, consuming the life of the survivor as they raged through time. Usually, and thankfully, it passed and they moved into an adjustment phase. This might involve some lowness of mood, anxiety, withdrawal and finally some sort of compact with life that allowed them to continue. The pain of the loss still felt but life continuing despite it. This was rather tritely termed acceptance. Robert mused how the counsellors in the Practice had formal psychological support for their work. The impact of the distress other Health Care Workers experience and how this affects them was only really in its infancy he thought. Much was written about Care fatigue. Not much was done about it. It was still very much the wartime cry of "Keep Calm and Carry on" for GPs.

ROBERT

The pressures of the working day had changed over the years for Robert. Patients often seemed to think that their appointments were all he did, and 30-40 per day did keep him busy, but over the years this number stayed about the same: it was the other pressures that increased. His Practice still did 2 or 3 home visits per day and this combined with 100 electronic prescriptions to authorise, 30 letters to read, 4 phone calls to make, 50 test results to consider and then dictate his own letters and oversee his areas of the Practice organisation. Then you had to keep up to speed generally, have at least some time talking to colleagues and remember to breathe in between! He remembered a GP academic presenting the results of his research into what attributes medical students needed to complete a successful career as a GP. He had a long list: clinical expertise, good decision- making, good communication skills, a positive approach...it was a daunting list but he summarised by saying "being well organised was the critical factor".

Most letters arrived electronically – 1 type of letter never did. Robert thought every Doctor's heart missed a beat when they saw a solicitor's stamp on a letter. He was looking at one now. Sometimes it might be the GMC stamp. The General Medical Council was set up in 1848 to ensure practising doctors were registered and qualified. It was the regulatory body and had developed a reputation over the last 10 years of being heavy-handed, poor at communicating and uncaring. Great for a Medical Professional body! Robert opened the letter: it was a complaint.

Patients could make a complaint in a number of ways. Directly to the Practice, through a solicitor, through the NHS network or through the GMC. Some did all 4! GPs preferred direct complaints but some patients saw the in-house process as being a bit too cosy and not rigorous enough. Involving a solicitor made the process confrontational from the outset and the GMC – well they had their reputation to protect too. The NHS network could often facilitate the process but, with 4 different systems in play, no one of them was ideal to Robert's way of thinking. He knew research suggested most patients wanted to understand what had gone wrong, perhaps get an apology, and be reassured action was being taken to stop it happening again to someone else. All of that seemed entirely reasonable but the process often introduced adversarial elements and left all parties dissatisfied to some degree.

Robert read the letter. Most Doctors care enormously about the quality of care they provide and complaints strike at their core. Every year a number of Doctor suicides occur as a result of medical incidents and the complaint system's subsequent response. Robert knew that medical diagnosis, decision- making, investigations, referrals and the vagaries of illness made the clinical world of general practice an uncertain place to work in. One of the phrases he had heard over the years was "the map is not the territory". Most of us have had the experience of using a map, perhaps to find a Post Office, or more importantly a pub, only to discover the pub on the map no longer exists. In this situation we just can't have a pint; in medicine it can be more critical. Robert had been taught a way, a sort of map, which helped him to understand what his patients told him. Generally, it worked well but sometimes it failed. It was only a model of the real world and it had its limitations. Sometimes it let him, and the patient, down. Sometimes badly. Then there were his own limitations: things perhaps he could be better at, times when he was below par for whatever reason, days when the work pressure was huge. All of this contributed to the challenge of being a GP. To his mind it was what made the job worthwhile, but it had a sting in its tail.

The patients had gone for the legal route and the solicitor's letters never beat about the bush. "You are accused of gross negligence for failing to diagnose this patient's breast cancer during the appointment on 18th Feb". It carried on detailing how the delay had compromised the patient's treatment and worsened the prognosis. Robert read it in silence. He was upset. Most Doctors enter the profession with what some term "a vocation". It means a calling. They want to make a difference to peoples' lives and are prepared to work hard to achieve this. They don't set out to make mistakes, they don't set out to upset patients, they don't set out to fail. Sometimes Doctors burn out. They can get "care fatigue" and in today's NHS, the incredible pressures can create this state. If this is not recognised then these doctors are more likely to make mistakes. Rates of depression, alcohol and drug abuse and divorce are all above average in the profession. When he qualified Robert was told he would have 2 significant complaints in his 30-year career. He was not superstitious but touched wood when he was reminded that this proved to be true for him. In the Modern NHS the complaints rate was more like 1-2 every 1-2 years. Medical interventions had expanded, increasing the potential for the right, and the wrong treatment, and the public were much more health aware with a lower threshold for complaints in society as a whole. The profession now ran courses on "resilience" to try and toughen up the profession to cope in this changed world.

Robert sighed. He looked at the patient's medical record and was surprised to see there was no consultation on the day it mentioned, although there was 1 a few years before where he had examined the patient's axilla. There was no mention of breast lumps until recent times when the patient had seen another Doctor and had a cancer diagnosed. He was a bit confused now. What was the patient's complaint based on? Like all practising doctors   Robert belonged to a Medical Protection Society. Essentially this is a body designed to insure and defend doctors, appropriately, in complaints processes. Robert phoned his society. They asked him to draft a reply to the solicitor pointing out that no consultation had occurred on the day stated and run it past them before sending it on.

Robert had a day's work to do. The wording of the complaint echoed in his mind all day. Complaints made him aware of his fallibility and decision making became that much more difficult. It often took weeks, or months, for that effect to subside. His 1 major complaint had taken more than 2 years to resolve and he had almost played it out in his mind on a daily basis. He would just be trying to adjust and another correspondence would bring it all flooding back. It had been a difficult time.

He sent the letter off and was generally able to forget what seemed a fairly straightforward misunderstanding. Another letter arrived. The Solicitor wrote "the absence of notes regarding the consultation on the 18th Feb is further evidence of negligence and we continue to prosecute our case". He almost dropped his coffee. He was known to be a stickler for note keeping but was also aware that rare events occur, even if rarely. He believed good Doctors questioned their actions. Could he have failed to record this consultation? The Medical Protection Society confirmed the solicitor was determined to continue the case. Robert was flummoxed. It would now be his word against the patient. He had no memory of ever seeing this patient let alone on that date. If the patient confidently asserted he had, in a courtroom, how would that pan out?

He had a few sleepless nights wondering what would happen next and then the pressures of work meant life had to carry on and he started sleeping better. Then he awoke at 4am with a jolt. He ran downstairs and got last year's diary out. There it was. On the 18th Feb, by complete luck, he had been on a course in London surrounded by 50 colleagues who could act as witnesses. He phoned the Medical Protection Society at 8.30am and told them. He sent them a copy of the course register to prove his assertion. The case collapsed. Robert did ask if he might get an apology for the anxiety he had been caused. That caused amusement down the phone - but no apology!

Robert reflected that the patient had probably genuinely mis-remembered and conflated an appointment 4 years ago that was not related to the breast cancer with their current problem. They had been diagnosed with a life-threatening condition with all the distress that involves and believed they had been let down by him. It seemed part of the job to accept the grief-like anger that patients would sometimes direct at him. Sometimes with some justification, sometimes with none. Then, was it part of his job to help patients through this process? Even if he felt targeted in a personal way? Very few complaints are deliberately malicious he thought. Time for his next patient.

JIM

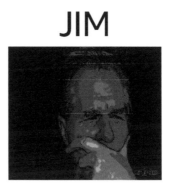

It was 6 months since his Dad died. The sadness was still there but the everyday pain of loss he had felt for the first few months was subsiding. He still felt the sudden urge to ring his Dad to give him some snippet of everyday news some days but even that was getting less. Christmas had been a bad time but now it was January. He was thinking about giving up smoking.

Robert knew there would be a trickle of New Year's resolution consultations against the tide of virus' and the possibility of flu. Sometimes he thought January was like being in the trenches with wave after wave of patients flooding the surgery. He was

aware the average New Year resolution lasted until the 12th January. His favourite resolution quote was from an American basket-ball player: "One year I vowed never to make New Year resolutions and I've stuck to it ever since".

Jim came in for review of his blood pressure and was just leaving when he stopped and said "Have you got any help for giving up smoking?". The "hand on the door" phenomenon again! "Definitely" replied Robert. "Sit down a second". Smoking remained one of the main causes of illness that Robert saw. If he managed to help Jim stop it might be one of the most important things he achieved that day.

Robert was taught about the Cycle of Change. Like most medical models the authors liked long words! It started with the pre-contemplation stage ie the patient didn't even think about the issue. The next was contemplation where they were consciously thinking about it. Jim was here by the looks of it. Then there was the action phase where patients started doing something, followed by the maintenance phase where, hopefully, they continued with the healthier behaviour. Finally, there was the relapse phase: many patients needed to go around the cycle a few times before they were permanently "maintained"! Doctors often try and move the patient around the cycle to at least the next phase. Sometimes Robert would say something a bit shocking to a smoker to try and get them to think. "I hope I don't ever see you with lung cancer" was quite a shot across the bows. Many GPs do courses on motivational interviewing. This technique is designed to allow the Doctor to explore the reasons why the patients might still be smoking, the hurdles that need to be overcome and the gains that could be achieved. The technique encourages the patient to identify the first steps that seem achievable against a real timescale. Sadly, as the pressures of more and more consultations have developed, these sorts of consultations are rarer, for GPs anyway. Robert had done a course on "Logical Levels" which was another technique for exploring behaviours developed by Gregory Bateson. If a patient wanted to stop smoking it might be the environment that is the issue, he may smoke in the pub with his mates. It maybe he needs to look at his behaviour – why is he smoking? Is it his choice? Why? Next, he may need to consider if he is capable of giving up smoking? How much help might he need to become capable? He may find he has beliefs or values around smoking that need challenging. "Everyone in the pub smokes" "I'll look stupid in front of mates" "They'll tease the hell out of me if I fail". He may need to challenge his identity as a smoker and finally it may even impact on his spirituality. Not a religious concept here but asking himself what he hopes to gain at a deeper level. These ideas often provided Robert with a few short interventions he could use to encourage positive change.

Jim had been shaken by his father's death and this had changed his attitude, perhaps even at the spiritual level, to smoking. He was very motivated to change and Robert booked him into the Nurse clinic. Sometimes he used to tell patients "I'll eat my hat if you change". A safe bet, he didn't have a hat! Often the patients had not really come for a lecture on giving up smoking or losing weight and there was only a certain amount Robert could achieve. Sometimes he remembered about the idea of locus of control. Patients might have an internal locus of control and accept it is their responsibility to change, or not change. Robert was surprised how many patients had an external locus and behaved as if their lives were really dictated by other factors. It was often quite difficult to help these people change.

"Would hypnosis help?" asked Jim. Robert smiled. He was aware of the alternative or complementary (amusing how many people put complimentary!) medical approaches to health care. There was some evidence that hypnosis might help, and acupuncturists, herbalists and a myriad of other practitioners were around with offers of help. One local shop window had a sign advertising a 100% cure for something. That annoyed Robert. If he made those sorts of claims the GMC would be after him! About 10 years earlier the concept of Evidence-based Medicine (EBM) was in a sense reborn. Patients might find it incredible that there is perhaps little, or poor, evidence for many mainstream treatments. Many operations and orthopaedic devices (knees, hips etc) are not really trialled in a meaningful way. Over the years the concept of EBM matured realising that research was a bit more difficult than it seemed. Evidence came in different qualities, some of it not very good. However, over time the situation improved but

it still galled Robert that many of the complementary special-
ties had not grasped the nettle. They needed to try and provide
better evidence of their efficacy. The Practitioners were usually
kind, caring and very genuine but was that enough? He was usually non- committal when asked about this and had himself done
some homeopathic courses in his time so was far from closed
minded here. He often thought about the power of the placebo.
He remembered being told that about a third of patients would
improve with a tablet of sugar. Particularly if it was red! He often
wondered how often his active medications were actually acting
as placebos and not really doing anything at all! Hopefully no
side- effects either. In the history of medicine placebos had probably been the most effective medicine! Nowadays actively using
one was seen as unethical, perhaps fooling the patient a bit. Robert wondered if the profession might be missing something here?

Some patients seemed happy to run the risks of poor health behaviours. Robert rarely met anyone under 30 who took the concept of death seriously. If he wanted to get a teenager to think
about giving up smoking, he might talk about how much it cost,
how it gave you wrinkles or point out how the advertisements
were designed to manipulate them. Some patients would consider the risks of treatment outweighed the gain. He remembered
a woman with very high blood pressure who would not consider
treatment at any cost. Life is a risk he mused.

Jim saw the Nurse in the Practice "Help2quit" clinic. In recent
years the number of these clinics had mushroomed. Some patients came for a "Health check" trying to stop a disease developing at all. Doctors called this Primary Prevention. This would
usually boil down to lifestyle advice on diet, weight, exercise and
cholesterol level. Robert's Practice, in line with common practise, used the "Qrisk" calculator that predicted a patient's percentage risk of having a stroke or heart attack over the next 10
years. As time went by Robert was advised to treat patients with
increasingly lower risk levels – 20% first, then perhaps 15% or
even 10%. This usually involved prescribing drugs called statins

to lower a cholesterol level, and thus lower their risk. The main problem was that almost everyone over 60 had at least a 10% risk factor! Not everyone wanted to take a statin and he, like most of his colleagues, shared his patient's ambivalence around this advice. He remembered a wordy quotation from a man called Shrebeneck; "The Roads to Unfreedom are many: one of them is labelled Health for All". How far should the Profession, or the State, go in the pursuit of a healthy population he wondered. At what point does it start to infringe individual freedoms? There was a danger of turning everyone into patients. Was his profession empire building?

Jim successfully gave up the cigarettes. A good job I don't have a hat, thought Robert.

BLACK DOG

R obert found the start of the year a challenge. The grey, leaden skies of cold January days brought a host of viral infections. February brought relief but also its own sort of epidemic: depression. Robert had seen the tides of depression ebb and flow over the years. GPs had been castigated in the 1990s for failure to diagnose the condition, then hauled over the coals for overdiagnosis and over-treatment in the new millennium. Now it was back to under-diagnosis. Sadly, the profession seemed a bit confused and unsure how to deal with this modern epidemic.

Robert had been taught about 2 sorts of depression: endogenous and reactive. The first a more serious internalised type of illness. The latter less serious and a reaction to overwhelming life events. Even then he had seen this as an over-simplification and had argued with a Professor of Psychiatry about it in a viva. Probably not a good place to argue but he passed – just! Depression seemed to be a disease of losses. Loss of interest, loss of mood, loss of libido, appetite and weight. Worse still loss of friends, career, partner and worst of all loss of life. More than half his surgery on a February morning could be depressed patients. Many patients did not recognise this as their problem. Depression could affect patients in a myriad of manners causing just about any pattern of symptoms you would care to think of. Some Doctors used questionnaires to diagnose the condition and Robert had tried this in the past. They could be useful to help a patient understand and accept the diagnosis but they could also come across as rather dismissive, impersonal and even intrusive tools. The stigma of depression in a society that struggled to understand what it meant and associated it with simple sadness made the diagnosis a challenge at times. Couple this with, in Robert's view, the disaster of Descartes, made it all rather a mess. Descartes was the one who decided you could separate mind and body. Sadly, bodily diseases somehow assumed an air of respectability and the mind ones didn't. Robert had yet to find a mind without a body or vice versa.

Robert had seen doctors manage depressed patients in a variety of ways. It was possible to elicit the symptoms, diagnose depression, issue antidepressants and arrange counselling in 10 minutes. Possible, but rarely satisfactorily. Many patients had "psychomotor retardation". A fancy medical term for thinking and acting slowly. They needed time to express themselves, time to think and time to react. Time is possibly my most precious commodity thought Robert and the temptation to cut time corners very alluring. Most of all he thought these patients needed to feel listened to. They wanted someone to understand how they felt. How much he really could understand was a question Robert often asked himself. Society often equated depression to some sort of severe sadness, failing to understand the qualitative difference between this and depression. Depression seemed to penetrate his patients' minds, bodies, lives and perhaps souls in a pervasive, invasive and destructive manner. Like many GPs, Robert had suffered mild depressive episodes and had some understanding that did help establish a relationship with patients, many of whom had struggled to get to their appointment at all. Robert felt they needed a supportive human being more than a technically proficient clinician.

The numbers of patients with depressive symptoms seemed to increase as the years went by with no sign of waning. Modern society and social media seemed to him to be part of the problem. Patients were constantly bombarded by images of what success and happiness should look like, what they should look like, how their existence should be validated and constant pressure to be more, have more, earn more and spend more. Idealised models of lifestyle, relationships and appearances were a constant pressure on vulnerable people. Robert wondered where all this led to for these patients. The medical model of depression was seductive. Antidepressants did help many patients, were easy to prescribe, and made both the patient and the Doctor feel they were doing something positive. The increase in Talking therapies like counselling and cognitive behaviour therapy (CBT) seemed a step forward but waiting times for these were often months. Patients who plucked up the courage to speak to their GP did not want to wait months for help and would often opt for antidepressants. Most GPs, like Robert, had ambivalent feelings about these drugs. They often seemed to help to a degree but did not address all the underlying issues that were part of the patient's depression. CBT encouraged patients to look at how their thoughts, feelings and actions all combined to colour their lives and Robert thought it offered real potential for change. If often took some while before patients were ready to accept this as a way forward and in the mean-time he tried to be a small cog in the machinery of their lives and help them along the way with whatever means he could find.

Robert often walked his black Groenendael dog and remembered Churchill's depression and description of this as his own Black dog. Some historians argued that without his depression Churchill would never had been such a great leader. In his own world it was difficult to see depression as an asset.

LORA

R obert had realised that life as a GP could be very different in different places. In some areas more than a third of patients moved every year. In his area it was only a handful. In some Practices they might have 20 languages to deal with. He had a mostly English-speaking list of patients. He had calculated that his whole list-size of patients would fit into a single tower block like the ones he could see as he drove through Birmingham. He sometimes drove 12 miles to see one patient. Life could be very different. Once he was tempted by an advert for a job on the Scilly Isles. That sort of experience would have been poles apart from inner city medicine. His semi-rural Practice sat somewhere in the middle of all this. Many people, often the City dweller, had the image of life in the country as some sort of rural idyll. Robert had pockets of severe deprivation in his countryside. He called it the fourth world – a forgotten place of squalor, subsistence living, poverty and illness. Not quite the inner city but having its own challenges. But not today. His next patient was Lora.

A particular local company had not been able to recruit staff locally for what were quite hard, physically demanding, dirty jobs. Their problem was solved with the hard-working attitudes of a significant Bulgarian community. The Practice now had hundreds of Bulgarian patients. They came from a particular area of Bulgaria where education was not readily available and foreign language teaching, other than Russian, completely absent. These patients spoke little or no English and made Robert's life interesting at times, to say the least. Needless to say, his Bulgarian wasn't very good either!

Thankfully most patients now brought an interpreter, usually a member of the family, sometimes a friend and occasionally a paid interpreter. The extra dynamic this introduced in the consultation could be a challenge. The family members who learnt English were often the children, often primary school aged, and they were then brought as the go-between. Conducting a consultation with a parent through an 8-year old child about what might be a very adult theme was a fraught affair. The child's understanding and interpretation of even simple questions was often, well, child-like. Sometimes Robert would deliberately ask closed questions hoping for a yes or no answer. There would then be a protracted parent-child conversation involving consternation, confusion and all sorts of other body language cues followed by a "yes" from the child. It left Robert a bit bewildered. Once one mother brought her 9-year old son to ask about menstrual issues – it was not really a success. To make matters even more interesting a Bulgarian nod meant no and a shake of the head was yes. Robert couldn't even rely on the normal body language cues. The NHS did provide a telephone-based interpretation service where you could ring and put the person on speaker phone and have a 3-way conversation. This worked better generally but was not always available and was always time consuming as Robert spent 10 minutes awkwardly looking at his patient whilst they both listened to Green Sleeves and waited for someone to arrive at the other end of the line.

Lora had a rash on her hands. She was worried that it was an infection and would stop her working. Robert, and just about every GP he had ever met, had completed Belbin's Team Inventory. It described the way you tended to interact in a team and had 8 categories. Many were obvious like the chairperson, the monitor or completer-finisher, some a bit less so like the resource investigator, shaper or even plant. The latter not of the garden variety but a slightly disruptive character that would challenge the team with innovative, if not particularly practical, suggestions. The course Robert had done focused on the GPs there but Robert found this model useful with patients too. Lora seemed to be very people-orientated and had been promoted to a supervisor role. She was anxious not to let her team down: she was a team worker at heart, another of Belbin's descriptions. Lora had a rash and, with limited English, thrust her hands at Robert. Thankfully she had mild contact dermatitis and could work whilst her treatment took effect. Robert wrote out a few bullet points for her that included the diagnosis, how to use the treatment, what to expect and when or whether she might need to come back. He didn't do this routinely for English-speaking patients but thought she might either get other family members to explain this or perhaps look it up on the internet. Robert recalled that the human brain really only takes in about 5 items during an explanation and tried to keep his written list to the same sort of number.

Many of the Bulgarian patients went home to see family on a regular basis. During these trips they would often see a Bulgarian doctor for a first or second opinion about their conditions. Robert was not surprised by this: often these consultations had a slightly unsatisfactory feel to them perhaps with certain questions unspoken and unanswered. However medical practice varies quite a lot from country to country. The French have the "crise de foie" or liver crisis which we don't recognise at all. The Germans treat low blood pressure which is pretty unheard of here and patients returning from Spain often had 4 medications for an ear infection where Robert would have struggled to suggest one at all! The

Bulgarians would then come home with medication they were told to continue. Sounds simple but this medication was often not available in the UK and was written in the Cyrillic alphabet! Often the chemical name would get Robert out of jail in terms of what the drug actually was. However, it was often difficult to explain that, in British medicine, this drug was not used for the condition they had. Robert imagined how the patients felt: their well-known and trusted Doctor, speaking their own language, was suggesting a particular drug. The British doctor with whom you could not really communicate, seemed to be saying you can't have it! He remembered some research showing that some immigrant patients actually thought they would be offered a lesser treatment than British-born patients. Robert tended to try and address this idea directly so as to stop that thought but it was a potentially difficult conversation.

Robert remembered a story he had been told many years before by an Army gynaecologist. A corporal had married a German girl and she had been told by her German gynaecologist she needed an operation and also told how much it would cost. Her husband then told her "that's fine, I'm in the Army and the Army Medical Service will cover you too". They arranged an appointment. After listening to her and examining her the Army Consultant said "Good news, there is an alternative to surgery that I think will be better for you". "But my German gynaecologist says I need an operation" she replied. The Consultant sighed and then explained, in some detail what the treatments were and why he recommended the non-surgical option. "But my German gynaecologist says I need an operation" she repeated. Another sigh from the consultant who paused and thought for a moment. "Perhaps I am explaining this from the wrong angle" he continued "How much is your gynaecologist going to charge?". "1000 marks" (this is an old story) she replied. "Now listen carefully" he said as he looked directly at her smiling "You do not need an operation.....but I will do it for 800 marks". An apocryphal tale perhaps thought Robert but sometimes the profit motive did seem to skew the thought process.

Lora was pleased with her prescription. She actually needed one, thankfully, because Robert had discovered that most of his Bulgarian patients expected the consultation to end with a prescription. Most patients had come to understand that there was no "pill for all ills" and accepted this fairly regularly. However, Robert suspected this was not the case in many other countries and this led to expectations. He wondered if the profit on the medications was, sadly, a part of this trend. Sometimes when Robert had finished the consultation, the patient would just sit looking at him and seemed to be thinking "If I wait long enough, I'll get something"!

When he had started his career 37 years earlier 5-minute appointments for GPs were common. There was even a revolutionary book published in the 1980s entitled "Six minutes for the patient" – wow a 20% increase! This had seemed a ridiculously short time period to him even then. On a course he was doing he challenged one of the lecturers about the Six Minutes book and received a rather condescending "poor young man, you'll learn" reply. Time had proved him right. First 7.5-minute appointments, then 10 minutes, and now, in some Practices, 15 minutes or more. This was double-edged though. As the population ages demand rises and, combined with GP shortages, workload increases. Offering longer appointments becomes a real organisational challenge. Practice Managers are left with the dilemma of running longer waiting times or accepting a fall in the quality of care. Robert remembered a colleague asking a group of 100 GPs "Who is going to specialise in the care of the elderly?". A scattering of hands went up. "What are the rest of you actually going to do then?" he retorted. Robert had once done a long-term locum in a very rural setting. Even then seeing anyone under 60 in the surgery was almost unusual. Many Practices have collapsed as Doctors retired and workload overwhelmed the ones left. There was a glimmer of hope that the new world of e-consultations might help fill the gap and Robert felt this might well meet the needs of patients with single-issue, uncomplicated problems. He also felt that continuity and the face-to-face consultation would remain essential. The world might change but human needs would not.

ROBERT – EPILOGUE

R obert had retired 6 months now. As a schoolboy he had been a competitive 400 metre runner. Some-how he had always seen this race as a bit of a metaphor for his career. 60 odd seconds to cover 40 years might seem a bit odd to many he thought but it worked for him.

You started on the blocks, with colleagues all around you. You were apprehensive, excited, challenged. How would the race go? Were you ready? Were you fit? Bang, the gun went and you were off. Nerves go a bit and it's time to keep up with the others, maybe even get ahead. As the first corner of the 1 lap race passes you feel fit as you accelerate and enjoy the race. Then the back straight; it always seemed more than 100 metres long. You try to settle into a good stride pattern. You're up to speed now and need to maintain it. Try to relax and feel competent, whilst building your place in the race. In his career this was where the postgraduate exams occurred. Now the final bend and the stagger unwinds. You become aware of the other runners and where you are in the race. It's a tough sprint for 400 metres and everyone is now struggling a bit. Then the final straight. You are encouraged – you see the tape in the distance. At 50 metres the pace is telling and its only stamina, experience and momentum that carry you to the line. You're exhausted.

How had he done? In a race he aimed to either win or run a PB – a personal best time. Just like a 400 metre race his career had involved good sections and ones where it was a struggle. He felt he had done his personal best and that was enough.

With retirement had come serious illness. Doctors often behave as if illness is something that happens to other patients and not them. The profession is renowned for over- and under-diagnosis, over- and under investigation, over- and under-treatment. Symptoms are either ignored or 2 and 2 are added to make 10! Self-treatment is common. The old saying that a Doctor who treats himself has a fool for a patient and a fool of a Doctor is often forgotten. Robert tried not to fall into these traps.

Robert knew that being ill was a traumatic experience: it changed things. Many of his colleagues used their own experience of illness to express empathy with patients. This could backfire. In some way all our experiences are unique and it could be tempting to feel that your own powerful emotional and physical response to illness was somehow universal. Patients could feel marginalised in a way completely contrarily to what their Doctor was trying to achieve. It was a tool to be used judiciously. Robert had often used the analogy of renal stone pain to explain this to students. You might have read all there was to know about this pain. The day you experienced the pain would change all of that in a moment.

Robert was grateful that patients had usually understood that he was human, with all the frailties, failings, ambiguities and imperfections that that entailed.

PART 2

A Family Doctor

I had planned to stop writing at this point. But it then occurred to me that some budding medical student might read this book. So, I have unashamedly written a brief chapter about my career in the hope of stimulating interest in General Practice. It has been a stimulating, challenging, varied and exciting 41 years and yet does still not touch the colossal variety and flexibility of career that I have seen colleagues achieve. They say a successful career should contain three components, the three "C's": Challenge, Commitment and Control. GPs manage more than 90% of cases they see, without tests or referral and entirely on their own: the patient does not normally see any other clinician. A Hospital Consultant might examine your chest but then you'll have a chest X-ray which sort of makes the examination pointless. GPs are the last bastion of clinical medicine – just you and your stethoscope against the world! If this isn't a challenge, I'm not sure what else is. GPs still have more control over the shape of their career than the Consultant in Hospital. This explains the incredible range of interests, clinical and non-clinical, that I have seen in my colleagues. Everything from working at Consultant level in Secondary care through to climbing mountains to investigate altitude sickness, running an organic farm or building their own home. This potential often inspires incredible commitment. It's been a privilege to work with these sorts of people.

If this sounds interesting then just don't take my word for it – give it a go!

Introduction

A Medical Student in 2015 says "No-one wants to be a GP". That made me feel immensely sad. I have been privileged to spend 35 years as a GP. It is immensely challenging: patients present with no end of symptoms that are not in the books, you have to try and keep up to date across the whole field of medicine and help run your own small business. You get to know your patients, some of them as friends, and you share the highs and lows of their humanity. Rarely you save a life, often you help life's progress and you become an important part of your patient's life. If "no-one wants to be a GP" then something has gone very wrong in our Medical Schools.

This section is an indulgence. It tells the story of a career with all its challenges and excitement. If one Medical student reads it and realises what a career as a GP can be like then I will be immensely pleased. If you just enjoy my story then that is fine too.

Beginnings

I started saying I wanted to be a doctor when I was 4 or 5. Relatives used to tell me this. Medicine is often a bit of a familial "illness" with sons and daughters following Mums and Dads. There was no Medicine in our family and I have no memory of some Damascene event that led to this ambition. I remember being interviewed by a student teacher practising interview techniques. He asked the obvious question: "Why do you want to be a doctor?" I told him I could give the answer he was expecting: I was interested in disease and the sciences, I was interested in caring and it seemed a good thing to spend one's life doing and all of this was true, but the deeper truth was that I had always wanted to do this and didn't really know why.

I do owe a debt of gratitude to the careers master at my comprehensive school. He was not liked, by any student or teacher I think, and was moody and curt. We all thought he was a drinker. Careers interviews were one sided affairs. "What do want to do with your life?" he asked. "Medicine" I replied. "What else?" he immediately retorted, in an almost cynically amused tone. Even by his standards this was a bit brutal. Now, I didn't really have a plan B so if he thought Plan A was unlikely things had to change. I started working harder from that point onwards. So thankyou Mr N.

Medical School

It's one of the truisms of life that you start at the bottom, rise up, move on to the next stage and then start at the bottom again. Medical School was, and still is, generally a 5-year degree course. I felt that God had been particularly kind in my A levels and included questions I could answer. If the physics papers had been more on electronics and less on mechanics I would have struggled. Consequently, when I arrived at Southampton Medical School I felt I was an imposter. I was surrounded by these clever colleagues, most with Public School educations and the confidence that goes with it. I worked hard and after the first term we had a series of examinations. Now, in those days there was no sensitivity to sharing everyone's results publicly: all the results, pass or fail, were put up on a notice board at the end of a long corridor. Everyone strained to get a look at their, and others, results. I fought my way through the scrum and found myself looking at my results; all As. I was shocked. I looked around and, I am a bit embarrassed to admit, thought "what a load of charlatans!". I learnt that confidence and ability were not the same thing. I also learnt I did not have to work quite so hard!

I chose Southampton because it was new. The course included what was termed "Early Medical Contact". This meant you met patients even in your first year. In many *traditional Medical Schools it was at least 2 years, sometimes even 3, before you set eyes on a real patient. I remember spending an afternoon with a 13 years old diabetic boy. He knew more about diabetes that I did! What I did learn was how this illness affected the life of a teenage boy. That lesson, and many others that year, stayed with me throughout my career. No-one had qualified from Southampton when I started and I remember a meeting to discuss what the degree was going to be called. Many Medical Schools awarded titles like MB ChB or BM BS. These were essentially qualifications in Medicine and surgery. There was a school of thought to modernise these older degrees and to award a simple BM – Bachelor of Medicine. I argued that if I was to do a 5-years degree I'd like more than 2 letters! I was a first-year student - my degree is BM, like all Southampton graduates.

Some would say Medical School is partly a rite of passage. I felt I was well taught but must admit to misgivings at the start of the course. It has been said that doing Medicine in the 70s and 80s was like doing 25 O levels. You were expected to learn a lot of facts. I could not believe I was expected to rote learn the anatomy I was faced with, along with biochemistry and physiology. I could do it but, after A levels, it seemed a backward step. Anatomy involved dissection and real cadavers. I think this was the start of some of the "toughening up" process we all had to go through. Bodies preserved in formalin do not look very lifelike thankfully. The anatomy exams often involved a "spotter". The dissection room tables were placed around the outside of the room and various bits of anatomy were displayed with tiny flags in them. Each of us would start at 1 table and have 2 minutes to identify the flagged structure before a bell rang and we all moved around to the next table, and so on. On 1 occasion the invigilator signalled the end of the exam and then added: "All students remain where you are. If you found questions 30-40 difficult please remain behind. The person who moved the flags is not as clever as they think. By checking when the answers changed, we will identify you, and there will be consequences".

It was about 2 years into the course when I decided to apply for an RAF Cadetship. I had always been interested in the military (my father was a Naval Captain) and in flying particularly. I had decided I wanted to be a GP probably before I started at Southampton and nothing had occurred to change my mind. I found Hospitals depressing and intimidating all at once and did not want to spend my life in 1. The RAF would train me as a GP, probably travel me around the world a bit and possibly let me in a few jets – what could be better?

The Royal Air Force

My 5 years at Medical School passed quite quickly. I graduated on a Friday and got married the next day. I had 2 weeks in Greece and then started the 2 stints of 6 months known as House Jobs in a smallish Hospital in Bath. It was a bit of a baptism of fire. On my first day on call I admitted 22 emergencies. I did not have any cover from a "SHO" (Senior House Officer) so ran around like a headless chicken wondering what I'd let myself, and my patients, in for. I was contracted for 88 hours per week but it was not enough. In those days the Junior House Officer did all the donkey work so we had to take our own bloods, write all the forms, get all the X-rays for the ward round and any other task no-one else seemed to do! You often started work at 8am on Friday and finished at 6pm Monday, with about 4 hours sleep on the Friday, Saturday and Sunday nights. It was said the worst time to be ill was 6am Monday as the House Officer had been at work for 72 hours, was sleep deprived with other colleagues starting at 8am to help would be tempted to prevaricate. 1 colleague fell asleep talking to the patient who woke them up! Thankfully this has changed.

Hospitals in the 80s were very supportive. They usually had Doctors' Messes and breakfast was free after a night on call. There was a camaraderie around the Mess that made these working conditions tolerable. It might have been challenging but your colleagues were surviving and so could you. There are numerous incidents I recall. I was helping John, my surgical SHO, drain a rather large perianal abscess in the theatre when, just before he incised this pint-sized monster of an abscess, he said "You owe me a pint if any of this goes in my boots". I had the suction device ready but, just as he incised the area and a thick stream of yellow pus poured out somehow, I missed it! It did all but fill his boots. I bought him a pint! We were on the crash team for sudden collapses and I was allowed home to sleep as the Hospital accommodation was about 200m from the wards. On one occasion at about 6am my crash bleep went off. I slept with clogs by the bed and, in my freshly awakened, bleary, state I jumped out of bed and shot off to the ward. Now at 6am the ward is wide awake and I ran into the ward, not noticing that my rather lose pyjama bottoms were now almost around my ankles, with the ward Sister running behind trying to pull them up! And all the patients enjoying the scene.

Every Doctor has the occasional "Diagnostic coup" and they should be enjoyed. One afternoon I was asked to admit the wife of a Brussels politician. She was sent in by the consultant from another team but I was on call so was the first to see her. She had a cough and X-ray changes. The consultant was very excited about the fact they kept parrots (you can catch psittacosis from them) and there were a few international phone calls taking place that I, thankfully, was excluded from. Now, as a Houseman you took a very full history and did a full examination and I noticed her appendix scar had become inflamed. Now they say a little knowledge is a dangerous thing but, in this case, it was just what I needed. I only knew 1 cause of an old scar becoming inflamed: a disease called sarcoidosis. I wrote this down as my main diagnosis in her notes. The Junior House Officer was the bottom of the pile so our thoughts were often, if not quite ignored, then treated as relatively irrelevant. It was a few weeks later that I attended a meeting where cases were presented. This patient was discussed and the diagnosis: sarcoidosis. The Senior Registrar finished by saying: "And if we had read the Junior House Officer's notes at the start we would have saved ourselves a lot of time and effort".

My RAF career now started with Officer Training at RAF Cranwell. Doctors, Nurses, Clergymen and re-entrants were given a rather watered-down and civilised version of Officer Training for only 4 weeks as I remember. We were taught office procedure, marching, RAF etiquette and I think some attempts at leadership training. We were taught how to eat an apple politely and of course how to salute. It was a curious experience in a rather other-worldly environment that rather unsettled me. Thankfully the real RAF turned out to be a bit more normal! I remember wondering how I could tackle my chicken dinner in an Officers' Mess when only myself and a very senior officer were together. After chasing the carcass around my plate unsuccessfully I thought *sod this* and picked it up. "I wondered how long it would take you to do that" was the officer's retort!

I was stationed in Lincolnshire on a Vulcan Squadron. These cold war V bombers were iconic to see in flight and had been in service for longer than my life. When I was given the opportunity to fly in one I was cock-a-hoop. You had to do escape training in a simulator first and this was a bit less encouraging. The 2 pilots sat in a rather tight cockpit area with the rest of the crew sitting backwards in what was called "the black hole" behind them. The way in was through a hatch in the floor. You were connected to the aircraft via your oxygen tube, parachute line and communication line. Now if the aircraft ran into trouble you disconnected everything (except the parachute!), sat on the edge of the hatch and swung yourself out. The instructor reminded you to try and miss the undercarriage that might be down at the time! When you are 23 and about to fly in a Vulcan for the first time you don't really worry too much thankfully! We used to get accident reports to read about aircraft incidents. They were often fascinating, if a bit terrifying, at times. A Vulcan had run into trouble and had to ditch in the sea so the pilots headed out and told the other crew to jump. Sadly 1 crew member forgot to disconnect his oxygen tubing which had a locking mechanism. Even more sadly his communication line did disconnect so when the pilots did a final check "Everyone gone?" he could not reply. The pilots ejected and he as now dangling below a pilotless Vulcan heading for the sea.

He climbed back up using his oxygen line as a rope, into the aircraft, disconnected the line and jumped. He survived. My flight was thankfully less eventful. Rather nauseating at times but great fun.

Medicine on an RAF Unit involved looking after the Airmen and their families. We started each day with a "Sick Parade" of 5-minute appointments for an hour or so. I got very good at treating acne, minor injuries, coughs and colds, the occasional sexually transmitted disease and giving out a lot of contraception. We did 2 or 3 Aircrew Medicals a day with morning and afternoon surgeries. Visits were very rare. We were Occupational Physicians and did kitchen and workplace inspections. We were attached to a squadron and tried to visit them weekly at least. Pilots were a bit suspicious of the Medical Officer. They jealously guarded their "A1" health status and saw us as a bit of a threat to their flying status. Getting to know them personally was designed to help them see us positively.

Most Medical Officers did a basic Aviation Medicine course. It was fascinating. Our physiology is not really designed for flight and the course had various ways of demonstrating this. The "spatial disorientation device" was a black box that you sat in and it rotated about a pivot at one end. You had headphones and a dial that the operator could illuminate to tell you what the device was doing. You were asked to commentate on what you thought was happening. At first you felt the movement but then it seemed to stop. The operator showed you the device spinning rapidly but there was no relative movement in your semi-circular canal balance mechanism so your body thought you were still. The operator asked you to put an ear onto your shoulder and it felt for all the world that the box had tipped up on its end. You knew it couldn't but it felt like it had. This was because one of your semi-circular canals had been taken out of the plane of movement and another put into it. The effect was disorientation and pilots needed to lean that their senses were not reliable indicators of what was actually happening. We all had a go in a centrifuge spinning us to blackout. It was not a fairground ride! Your face sags, cheeks pull in and eyes droop. The Operator says everyone should spin their prospective partners to 6 G and see what they will look like in 30-years' time! You were strapped in and told to look straight ahead. 2 lights were either side of you in your peripheral vision and you were given a button to push every time these lights came on. If you did not "cancel" these lights the central light went red. Now as you spin faster with your head inwards your heart struggles to pump the blood into your head. Because of the normal pressure in your eye this is the first place the blood supply starts to fail. Suddenly the red light appears and you realise your vision has tunnelled to central vision only. Moments later you are still conscious but with no vision. The operator slows the centrifuge and it's a miracle – you can see! One of our number did go unconscious. We also went in a decompression chamber. We were taken to the equivalent of 20,000 feet or so, with oxygen masks on, and working in pairs. 1 of the pair was told to remove the oxygen and then start taking 7 off 100 serially. Your colleague goes an interesting blue colour quickly and starts doing the subtractions well. Most of us got to about the 51 mark and then, despite knowing what you were meant to do, the process wouldn't happen and, strangely, it was amusing. You got a tap on the shoulder to replace your oxygen mask at this point. Again, pilots are taught the dangers of deoxygenation and the signs to recognise.

My GP Training then continued, you might think bizarrely, with 6 months paediatrics in London. The RAF had a number of what they called attached posts to allow us to complete a recognised training programme. I was then posted to a base in Germany for the next 3 and a bit years. I joined 20 squadron that flew Jaguars, a single pilot fast jet bomber. The Medicine was similar to Lincolnshire with a lot of young children and a lot of gynaecological issues along with the constant minor trauma.

We were quite a large base – 5 doctors and about 7000 personnel. Every month or so we would "go to war". Sirens would go off, I would put on my protective kit and head off the to the "WOC" or War Operations centre. The whole base was now on exercise for a few days. There were mock casualty exercises, gas attacks and war reports. I found it difficult to take seriously at times. One of the events that was always tried was for an "intruder" to get into our facility. They usually failed and moved on but, on this occasion, I was lying on a stretcher bed dozing (exercises were often tedious for hours) when there was a sudden commotion and shouting in the adjacent room. "Hands up – stand against the wall" I heard. *Oh no* I thought *they've let the intruder in.* I listened for a minute or so and then realised the intruder did not know I was in the next room. Now, as an officer, I had a 9mm pistol and I thought *what would I really do?* The odds were that the intruder had an automatic weapon and my shots were unlikely to disable immediately and he would then open fire. But, what the hell, this was not real was it? So, I leapt, in my best John Wayne style, into the doorway and bang, bang, bang supposedly emptied my magazine into this intruder. "Up against the wall" he said. "No" I replied standing my ground, "You're dead". He was not having this but by now my colleagues had joined in and the whole scenario was over. On another occasion we were made to evacuate and then go to our secondary site, an unprotected building. As we went the tannoy announced "There is an imminent tactical nuclear strike expected" so I sat down. The Observer asked pointedly "What do you think you are doing?" I looked up at him: "The building I am assigned to has no useful protection at all so if a nuclear strike is expected I might as well sit here and watch it". I think perhaps it was then I realised a full career in the RAF was probably not for me.

As a large base Medical Officers from Bruggen were often sent to cover other bases. I had stints in Berlin, Sardinia and the Falklands. Berlin was still partitioned in those days and both fascinating and disconcerting all at once. Thinking of concerts, I was there when Queen did a Berlin performance and I saw 2 ruptured ear drums the next morning! On call was at the British Military

Hospital. One evening I remember stitching up wounds on 6 Scottish Highlanders that matched the corresponding wounds on the 6 of the Yorkshire Regiment I had in an adjacent room. The military policeman was taking a statement from me later and stopped. "How long have you been in the services sir?" he asked. "About 2 years" I replied "Why do you ask?" "You seem a bit surprised by this evening's events sir". "Well, we don't tend to beat the hell out of each other on a Friday evening in the RAF" I continued. "Ah, it's a different service sir" he said with no note of amusement or irony. A whole floor was kept empty for the Hospital's most notorious visitor. Rudolf Hess had been held in Spandau since the Nuremburg trials. He was even admitted when I was on call so, technically, I was his doctor. I never saw him: The Consultant took over. I think he was a rather pathetic figure by then. He committed suicide age 93 some years later. Often bases in Germany were ex German WWII bases. The Officer's Mess on 1 base had a turret where Goering liked to drink with his younger Luftwaffe pilots and tell stories of his WWI exploits. By all accounts these were not entirely true and he apparently used to say "If this is not true may the roof fall in on me". It looks like German pilots are a lot like British ones. They like a joke and some of them rigged a device to drop the roof a few inches as he said this! It was still working in 1984 – I had a go! Whilst we were in Berlin my wife and I went through to the East. In uniform I was entitled to go with no restriction. I did not even have to prove my identity at Checkpoint Charlie. We went to the Opera and I was in full dress uniform. I could not see any other NATO officers in the audience. I saw quite a few East German border guards and Russian Officers. At the interval the guards were coming in small groups to see the "decadent" western officer until a Russian Naval Officer shooed them away. After a meal we went to the eastern side of the Brandenburg gate and had it all to ourselves. That was until a guard goose-stepped up to me in a rather disorientating manner, saluted me rather crisply and gabbled in German. "Quick Jayne, I think we're off to Siberia" I nervously replied. My wife speaks German. He wanted us to move the car!

Sardinia and the Italians were a interesting experience. We used a base where pilots could practise air to air combat in a "Top-gun" type environment. The Italian Airforce was, not surprisingly really, different. I saw an Air Traffic Controller enjoying a gin and tonic on duty for example. We had our own Air Traffic Officer there (not surprising I hear you think). He was half Italian and well known locally. We went out for a squadron meal and he pro-duced 2 bottles of orange liquid with wires protruding from the cork. The owner of the restaurant appeared and asked if he could get more. It was filu di ferru distilled illegally and the bottles bur-ied. You found them by the wire protruding from the cork and above the ground.

It was typical of the high alcohol hooches you get in hot Mediter-ranean countries and generally ripped you apart from mouth to stomach as you drank it! I ate mussels that evening. During the en-suing night I started itching, my eyes swelled and I was covered in an allergic rash. You can imagine how a squadron of young pilots reacted. They thought it hilarious that the "Doc" was unwell. They went back and framed the menu, complete with their com-ments, and presented it to me. I've never had mussels since. On 1 occasion I was living on the "Married patch" in Sardinia. This was just a few rented houses in an Italian village. The local sanitation was a bit suspect as was the wine delivered to your door by a rus-tic sun-dried Italian of indeterminate age and red teeth. Every Wednesday a sample of the local water was sent to our hospital in Germany to be tested. I was warned what could happen, and it did! The pathologists in Germany could see suspicious bugs in the water and they tell the Medical Officer – me this time. I then have to arrange a bowser of clean water to supply our families. The lo-cals see this and, in true Italian style, flock around the bowser noisily. The local landlords then demand an explanation from the Station Commander who phones the Medical Officer – me again. Inevitably, after a lot of angst and Italian emotionality countered by British Stoicism (more like thinly disguised terror on my part) the pathologists decide, after a few days, the water is OK really.

Everyone calms down. I rush back to Germany hoping never to set foot on Sardinia again. Actually, before we leave Sardinia completely there is 1 more tale to tell. "Have you every thrown a beer over an American?" I was asked by one of our pilots rhetorically. "Come with us, and bring your beer". We went to the bar and started talking to 2 American pilots drinking there. The conversation was manoeuvred to local tipples and Sambuca in particular. "You can drink this on fire" my colleague informed his trans-Atlantic allies. He ordered 2, lit them and holding 1 aside drank the other quickly. Now if you let the sambuca burn down it heats the glass edge enough to make you flinch. So, after a time he gave this to his victim, nudging me at the same time. The American paused, making matters worse, and then drank spilling the sambuca down his front and lighting himself up in a rather interesting blue flame which was put out by my beer poured all over him. He was very grateful, even bought me another beer.

I went to work in the morning. By the afternoon I was aware I was going to the Falkland Islands for 4 months, in 2-weeks' time. This was 1982, a year after the conflict, unaccompanied and in tents in the South Atlantic Winter. Well I did say I wanted to travel at some point and when you join the services you sign up for what they serve up. I was not thrilled but had no choice. I was spared the journey by ship and flew in a Hercules from Ascension Island. This is a 13 hours flight in a cold, noisy aircraft with no views. On reflection all I would have seen was thousands of miles of sea anyway! We were living in tents on the airfield surrounded by the debris of war. It was cold but I had been left a thermostatic heater by my predecessor. The only problem was that as it turned on it had a habit of tripping our generator and then I would have to run to my tent and hide it. The electrician never did discover why our generator was so fickle! There was not a lot of medicine to do so my time was spent trying to update our facilities. My immediate boss explained: "There are 2 ways of getting things done here: the official way is my way and it doesn't work; the unofficial way is your way and I don't want to know how it works". I found out quickly what that meant. Portacabins were arriving by ship for all the various departments to move into. We were well down the pecking order for 1. I discovered that the system was to unload them, number them and then allocate them. We saw a ship pass into the harbour (thankfully they had to go right past the airfield) and we then headed off to Stanley harbour with a truck and a crane from some friendly engineer whose shoulder I had put right. We unloaded 4 portacabins and came back. They were never numbered and officially didn't exist! The only problem was that we had to put them up ourselves. It took 10 medics and a lot of hot air. Then we needed to light the area. I reasoned that no-one would miss 1 runway light, there were dozens of others. So, I took an end one. We had a very bright Medical Centre! Eventually, after arranging for 50 metres of road to be laid one night, my boss told me to calm things down a bit! Facilities were a bit basic. I had a bath once a week in the Stanley hospital and I was the lucky one. I remember sitting on a long bench, over a ditch, with holes cut out for about 5 of us as we shared our morning ablutions. Dinner was in "Scrandet" across the mud path, except when it all blew away 1 night! We ran a small social club and I sold sweets, booze and, to my shame, cigarettes. I tried not to make a profit by rounding up the NAAFI prices to the next penny but we still made a rather annoying profit and I wasn't sure what to do with it. I bought videos and TVs for other units until the NAAFI solved my problem. They realised I was undercutting them so proposed to close me down. I worked out how much stock I would need to last the 2 months I had left there and took 3 ambulances down to Stanley and stacked them to the roof. I remember trying to balance the stacks of beer as we trundled back the 4 miles of hardcore road. We stacked these all around the Medical centre. Unfortunately, this coincided with the visit of a photographer taking pictures for the bigwigs back home. The pictures included stacks of beer, whisky and cigarettes in almost every corner. "Which of these do you suggest I send back?" my boss asked with irritation. I did find a few he could use and took the rest away: I still have them. Life was a bit tedious at times and as they say Idle hands…I should have known better. We had a navigator who had been in the RAF for years and knew how to work the system. He had actually managed to get a motorbike shipped out and, as a motorcyclist myself, I was a bit jealous. I typed a letter summoning him to the Stanley Magistrates Court stating he was in contravention of the Falkland Road Traffic Act (there wasn't one) for having no road tax (you didn't need any). I heard nothing. Then one of the Admin staff came over for a coffee and, just as he left, asked "Do you have a typewriter here Paul? I've been asked to make a list, something about dodgy letters going around". I told him we did and started to stew. A few days later an RAF policeman arrived and asked me to certify that type print off our typewriter was genuine. My Sergeant seemed quite amused. I was less amused and now was worrying. They let me stew a bit more. A few days later I got a phone call from the Station Commander's PA saying I was wanted in his office, with my hat on. The latter phrase meant trouble. Station Commanders were God on their units, I was worried. I sat outside for what seemed like hours. What I didn't know was that the Station Commander was not there and, when I did go in with heart racing and sweaty palms, there was Ray (the navigator) smiling with s drink in his hand. "You need to choose your victims a bit more carefully" he laughed.

The 4 months passed and I spent quite a long time suturing minor injuries, treating acne and providing a bit of R and R for the troops generally. I flew home in the South Atlantic winter. The experience did change me. I had decided a career in the RAF was not for me and that I would leave after my Short Service Commission. I spent more than 6 months away that year and felt that was not the sort of family life I wanted.

My "perk" for the Falkland secondment was to go to "Red Flag". This was a flying exercise in the USA. The Jaguars were going to "bomb" the Arizona desert with the "Enemy" protecting it with fighter aircraft and "Smokey SAMS" missiles. These missiles shot straight up in the air, issuing smoke, indicating you had been targeted but not actually coming at you! We were billeted in Hotels in Las Vegas and I had 3 weeks of fun. We were even given "overseas allowances" ie more money to be there! Area 51 was in the middle of the exercise zone and pilots were told to strictly avoid this so I never found out about the aliens living there! Thankfully no-one crashed (they fly at 100 feet and 500 knots in this exercise) and we all returned home safely: 1 or 2 cases of gonorrhoea excepted! We did have a trip to the Grand Canyon. I went in a car with 3 pilots. There is really only 1 place you can get done for speeding on the route. Generally, the road is flat and you can see a police car miles away. There is 1 area by the hoover dam where you can't – we got caught. We had the quintessentially British pilot with us "I'll handle this" he said in his refined Public-School diction. The Patrolman was not impressed and it was not going well. It got worse. An ex school mate of mine, now a pilot, thought (probably didn't think at all now I consider it again) *this is boring, let's make it fun* "We'll give you 50 dollars more if you pull your gun" he announced. I thought we were all going to jail. The fine was quite expensive. From 56kph to 64kph was "abuse of energy" and quite a cheap fine. As soon as you hit 65 it went up with a jump and then was $5 more for every mph. We were doing 72. I think we paid about $90.

I finished 3 years in Germany and then did a few more hospital-based jobs and finished off my GP training. In those days the examination for the Royal College of General Practice was not compulsory but I decided it might help me get job interviews so gave it a go. The most interesting component was a viva where 2 senior GPs asked you a series of questions over about 40 minutes. This aspect of the exam has now been dropped as a bit of an unreliable assessment but I always quite enjoyed vivas. It was a bit like a game of tennis: they hit the ball to you fairly straight at first. How you returned it might determine how hard the "rally" became. I remember 1 question where I was asked about the management of a breast lump. After I had run through how I would assess and examine the lump the examiner interrupted: "The patient says she thinks you are wonderful and would you come on a date with her?" I was not expecting that and paused! "I gather this sort of thing does happen" I started "but it's never happened to me. I wonder why?" The examiner laughed, getting the examiner to smile was never a bad thing! I passed.

As I approached the end of my RAF career I was used as a sort of locum to cover various bases for short periods. I managed a few more flights in various aircraft amongst which was the most memorable. A pilot from my Jaguar days was now an instructor in RAF Valley and asked if I'd like a flight in a Hawk (the current Red Arrow display aircraft). I never said no to these offers so off I went. He let me fly the Hawk over N Wales. I did a loop, a stall, a spin and some low level-ish stuff. It was such fun! As I spun down from 28,000 feet he suddenly called "hands off" and took over. "We had about ½ spin and then no room to recover from hitting the ground, he later told me. The N.Wales countryside had still seemed quite a long way down but at 400 knots you go a long way quickly! I was glad he was there, at least at that point. "Now I have to practice 6G turns for a while" he said. The fun was over as he reeled left and right (sorry port and starboard) and the G suit I was wearing compressed my legs and stomach trying to keep blood getting to my head.

In 1987 there were roughly 200 applicants for every GP post in the South-west and around 100 in the Midlands. It was similar across the whole country. In 2017 posts remain empty and practices get 1 or 2 suitable applicants if they're lucky. Times have changed. I applied for over 100 posts, had 22 interviews and was offered 3 jobs. In the end we had to leave our RAF married quarters and we took a 6 months maternity locum in a Shropshire village of A.E. Houseman fame called Clun. "Clunton, Clunbury, Clungunford and Clun are the quietest places under the sun". Clun nestles in steep Shropshire hills with its 2-3000 inhabitants. The surgery, now a shop, was 1 room divided by hardboard walls with no running water. There had never been a type-written referral. We lived in a delightful stone cottage with ducks in the garden. It was idyllic. I owe a huge debt to the villagers. It was where I learnt how to care for the elderly. In the RAF I never saw anyone over 65. In Clun I rarely saw anyone younger. The patients welcomed us warmly and the 6 months there were a joy. I had every Thursday off to venture out into the big bad world job-hunting and then I would scamper back to my rural paradise. It was like living in Brigadoon, the rest of the world did not really exist. By the way the locals often misquote Houseman replacing "quietest" with "drunkenist". It still scans and has some truth to it as well.

Beware of staying in 1 area too long, the odds you will stay longer increase over time, and so it was. Being local I was interviewed in Oswestry. The interview went well and I was offered the job. It was just the sort of Practice I was looking for. A small market town in a semi-rural area with only 5 partners and a fairly stable population: just the place for family medicine. Patients often think of General Practice as a homogeneous career across the country and the core qualities are similar. But life for the GP in Tower Hamlets is poles apart from the one in Skye. I was looking for something in the middle. The Senior Partner asked me at the end of the interview "How do you think you will get on here?" "Well I've enjoyed meeting you all but I don't think we can know the answer until we start working together" I replied. He later told me the honesty of that answer contributed to them making the job offer. It had taken that 5-year old boy 25 years to start the job he had imagined.

Family Medicine

My 6 months' probation passed. We'd bought a house, had a baby and settled in. I felt all grown up at once! I got some wonderful pieces of advice from colleagues. One retired partner asked "How long will you stay here do you think?" and I replied "Probably my whole career I hope". "Give the patients what they want" he said. "That will get you a good reputation that will last, there will be time to change things later". General Practice in the 1980s was very different from in the new millennium. We had no computers, 1 part-time nurse, no practice manager, no real management systems for prescribing or staffing and we did all our own on call. We had a peculiar sort of A5 note card for records we kept in what were called Lloyd George folders. Yes – the Lloyd George of the 1920s! There was a very light touch of regulation, and standards across the country varied enormously. I was very lucky to be joined by another colleague after 4 months and over the next 5 years we changed the record system, the prescribing system, the staffing structure, introduced computerisation and moved into a new surgery. It was a bit of a golden era where Practices could implement changes fairly easily without the NHS being overly curious. The critical component in all this was that we all got on as a group. People would be surprised at how prickly relations between some doctors can become, and remain, like this for long periods. Finding a Practice mature enough to accept that people are different can be difficult. I once asked a colleague how long he thought a new partner takes to settle into a practice – 7 years he replied and I was shocked. Now I think he was right.

Social mobility in Oswestry was very low in those days, and probably still is in 2018. They say Shropshire is the graveyard of ambition. Once you arrive you stay. It's a nice place to live and bring up your family. I knew 4 generations of families and it was interesting how patterns of illness ran in these families. I am not talking about the diseases that can be passed down genetically but rather the way patients react to being ill. The anxiety I remember in grandma could be seen in later generations. The techniques that helped grandma over this worked for them too. I started to get a grasp of my medicine and how I wanted to practice.

There is no real career progression for GPs. You get a job and generally that's it. The progression that does occur generally follows a set pattern. The younger GP settles in and learns "to drive" ie a bit like when you pass your car test and only then do you really learn the reality of using the roads. This takes a few years and then they start to develop the capacity to take on more. It might be roles within the Practice (developing a clinical expertise in some area, minor surgery, helping run the Practice) or ones outside. I had become a GP trainer and looked after younger doctors doing their GP "internship" and enjoyed the stimulation that these enthusiastic people had and the challenges they presented. They kept you on your toes. Someone then suggested I perhaps become poacher turned gamekeeper and apply to be a RCGP Examiner. I looked up the process and applied. After being appointed I challenged one of the interview panel: "it said I wouldn't need to do the exam again when I applied but it appears I have really?" "Well you might not apply if we admitted that" came the reply with a grin. It was quite fun setting questions, doing vivas in London and Edinburgh twice a year (Christmas in Edinburgh is lovely: I recommend it) and attending an annual conference. I did it for 8 years and was very grateful to my partners in the practice for letting me have the time. Sitting across the other side of the table doing the vivas was the only activity I ever found that put me under more pressure than a surgery of appointments. You had 5 minutes on your subject to award a grade. You started with a stem question and then made it a bit easier, to see if they might fail, or harder to award higher grades. Then the time finished and your colleague was off on another topic. It was gruelling for both sides of the equation and needed a lot of concentration. I finished a viva once and realised I had missed marking one of my colleague's questions entirely! Candidates were usually anxious, occasionally angry and 1 even cried. Perhaps it is better these days with no viva. The exam evolved over the years and, in an attempt to assess consultation skills, candidates were asked to produce a 7-consultation video tape to be assessed. Trainees spent hours collecting their very best consultations and examiners were then closeted in rooms for 8 hours a day watching them. The completed tape was like an apprentice's masterpiece. I once heard how one of the trainee's husbands taped rugby special one night over his wife's recordings! I heard the marriage survived! Thankfully this idea was dropped and trainees now do a simulated surgery that I gather is still terrifying but does not require hours of tape editing any more.

Most GP Practices allow doctors to have a sabbatical period off work from time to time. This had never happened in our practice, generally because you had to fund it and your replacement while you were away: a costly affair. I approached various bodies for help and based my period of 4 months away on a study of training methods in General Practice. I did a survey of grass roots experiences and then spent 2 months in Sydney and 2 months in Vancouver adding to the survey and writing up my results. We built family holidays around the locations and I had a great time. I wrote up my findings in the form of a book and it sat in my office for months until a friend with publication contacts asked to see it. After some peer reviews and a bit of re-writing it was published and certainly helped fund my time away and may even have been useful for some of the many GP Trainers who, thank you, bought a copy.

During this period, I applied to be a "Course Organiser" for our area. This meant joining a small team to organise and run GP training in our county. It was a privilege to work with these highly capable and motivated colleagues and see scores of young doctors develop into GPs. I felt a bit of a fraud teaching groups of well-educated professionals and decided perhaps I should get an educational qualification. I had done a lot of courses with doctors and felt, like me, they were potentially "gifted amateurs" so I decided to do a course with teachers and, very slowly over years, I did a Master of Arts in Education. I wrote a few articles for the occasional journal, a chapter for another book and some local publications. All of this was a bit like icing on a cake and, amazingly, added to the day job as a GP. I was awarded a Fellowship of our College – or given an F as some put it (you go from Member of the Royal College of GPs – MRCGP – to Fellow – FRCGP).

I spent a period as an appraiser for colleagues performing the annual 3-hour interview all GPs now do annually and saw a pattern in the professional career. It seemed you spent 10 years learning your trade (roughly through your 20s), the next 10 perfecting and developing your style and expertise (your 30s), then you had

10 years of "peak practice" where you had the skills, energy and capacity to perform at you best. (now in your 40s). Then you had another 10 years to try and hang on as adapting to change became more difficult, energy levels lower and demands even higher. It seemed a bit of an irony to me that senior GPs were usually seeing at least as many patients as their 30-year old colleagues, often more of the elderly complex ones too, with added responsibilities within the Practice just as they were getting more knackered! As the retirement age increases I suspect this will change. General Practice has a good track record of adjusting to meet the workforce needs – the numbers of female GPs are testimony to that – but will need to do the same for the aging GP of the future.

Retirement

Eventually computers were my downfall. I had always resisted their increasing intrusion into both mine and my patients' lives. My working day started to become more computer centric and less person centred. I imagine that the next generation will find this less onerous and I constantly reminded myself that the core of my work had not changed. Patients came with a problem. I tried to help. Then, ironically on my birthday, all prescriptions were computerised so I had to spend another hour per day at least signing them off in my room, on my own, staring at a screen. I've read that some practices now have communal computer rooms so at least this can be a partly social experience but the bell tolled for me that day. I checked my pension at lunch time and was retired within the year.

It sounds like I've finished on a low note but don't misunderstand me. Turn the clock back 30 years and I would rush headlong in the same direction. It has been a wonderful experience, an honest-to-God privilege and I would do it again in a jiffy. The letters and gifts I got from patients and colleagues were humbling. I find it difficult to see how careers in Hospital Medicine, essential though they might be, can compare with the challenge, variety and potential that General Practice offers. Perhaps you should try it!

ACKNOWLEDGE- MENTS

M ost of this book was written during serious illness and I was only sustained by the constant care and support of my wife. Words cannot express how I feel about her. Thanks to the friends and family who read the book and gave suggestions.

The images are courtesy of free-images.com and modified with the clip2comic app.

My greatest thanks go to 2 other groups. Firstly, thanks to the dozens of colleagues I have worked with, from those first days in Southampton in 1975, through to those still supporting me as I retired in 2017.

Now, the most important group: most GPs will conduct more than 100,000 consultations with patients in their career. Some nearer to 200,000. I never counted all of mine but I think I probably learnt something from every one of them. Thank you all.

REFERENCES

I haven't tried to produce a comprehensive reference list: this book is primarily for patients. However, some people may want to look at some of the ideas in a bit more depth, and this brief list might be helpful.

Balint E (1984) The History of Training and Research in Balint Group. Journal of the Balint Society 12:3-7

Balint M (1957) The Doctor, the Patient and the Illness. London. Pitman

Balint E and Norrell JS (1973) Six Minutes for the Patient: Interactions in General Practice Consultation. Tavistock Press

Battles J et al (1990) The Affective Attributes of the Ideal Primary Care Specialist. In

Belbin M (1981) Management Teams. London. Heineman Press

Berne E (1977) Games People Play. Penguin. Harmondsworth

GMC (1999) Good Medical Practice. General Medical Council. London. HMSO

Hart JT (1992) Two paths for medical practice. The Lancet. Sep 1992 26:340

Helman D (1981) Disease versus illness in General Practice JRCGP: 31: 548-553

Honey P and Mumford A (1992) The Manual of Learning Styles. Maidenhead. Peter Honey

Horder J (2001) The First Balint Group. British Journal of General Practice 1038-39

Irvine D (1999) The Performance of Doctors: The New Professionalism. Lancet 33:9159:1174-1177

Marinker M (1996) Sense and Sensibility in Health Care. Wiley Blackwell

Mehrabian A (1971) Silent Messages (1st ed.) Belmont. Wadsworth

Middleton P and Field S (2001) The GP Trainers Handbook. Abingdon. Radcliffe Medical Press.

Neighbour R (1992) The Inner Apprentice. London. Kluwer Academic Press

Neighbour R (1987) The Inner Consultation. London. Kluwer Academic Press

O'Connor J (1993) An Introduction to NLP. San Francisco. Aquarian Press

Prochaska SO and DiClemente CL (1980) Towards a comprehensive model of change. In WR Miller and N Heather (eds) Treating Addictive Behaviours: processes of change. Plenum Press

Shrebeneck D (1992) The Death of Humane Medicine and the rise of Coercive Healthism. Social Affairs unit. London

ABOUT THE AUTHOR

Paul Middleton BM(Hons) MA (Education) FRCGP DRCOG DFFP Cert Av Med qualified from Southampton Medical School in 1980 at the age of 22. He spent almost 10 years as an RAF Medical Officer including tours in the Falkland Islands and Germany. He then spent 30 years as a semi-rural GP on the English/Welsh border. He retired in 2017.